The Wisdom of the Trees

by

Jen Ward

Uploaded through CreateSpace October 2017

ISBN-10: 0-9994954-0-2
ISBN-13: 978-0-9994954-0-7

CONTENTS

Introduction   5

The Wisdom of the Trees   7

About the Author   111

Other Books by Jen Ward   113

INTRODUCTION

There is a tragedy that plays out in this world of human interactions. It is that lack of regard and acknowledgement of the wisest beings on earth. Trees have stood watch as sentinels throughout history for the ignorance and follies of man. They have passed on their wisdom generation after generation through their sapling offspring. When a tree is felled, it folds its wisdom into the earth and rebirths it in a spray of seedlings. This wisdom is scattered throughout the world through the wind and animals.

The trees hold the mysteries of the history of the planet. They are eager to share with all who will listen. Not only do they exchange our discarded breath for fresh oxygen, they take all the stagnant energy of our anguish and convert it back into clarity and calm. This is another one of their unacknowledged gifts to us. Trees are directly related to the sanity in the world. The places that are the most imbalanced in the world are the ones with fewest trees.

There is no need to take anyone's word for this. Simply go outside and be present with the magnificent beings that serve unconditional love and resilience. Ask a tree any question. It will answer. Ask as if you are asking out loud without the need to speak the question. The tree will answer. You merely must awaken your subtle senses to listen. The answer will come as if hearing it within your own mind. As if it were your idea. This is how subtle the exchange is. May you awaken to the connection to these kindred spirits. As you do this, your life will be transformed and so will the world.

THE WISDOM OF THE TREES

What Love Can Do

I will listen to and help anyone I can regardless of whether it is a person, animal or foliage. Yes, plants speak as well as animals if someone is listening. If no one listens, I am not certain if they speak so much. Maybe they give up being heard just like people and pets do. Some of the plants at my friend's house tell me when she doesn't give them individualized attention. One was very thirsty and told me so. She got embarrassed and called it a tattletale as she watered it.

There was a grove of trees that I would commune with every day as I walked my roommate, Simha (a lab mix). They brought us both comfort for different reasons. At the end of the row was a medium-sized maple tree that was covered with grapevines. It was suffocating and kept from growing by the vines holding it down. I really wanted to get some of the grapevines off the tree because I have known for years that most trees don't like the vines growing on them (it's like wearing an itchy sweater when they are wrapped around their trunk), and these vines were killing this maple tree. It looked sick and had a lack of leaves on it because of them.

It was situated in a ditch with a few logs pushed up against it.

The groundskeeper used the area around the trunk to throw clippings and logs that were discarded from the manicured part of the property. It didn't look too bad to onlookers because it was all covered with the grapevines. Only the tree and I knew it was suffering. I could feel it asking for help and I wanted to help, but it was a little out of my comfort zone. After all, although it was neglected, it wasn't my property.

Daily, as I walked by this tree, it would encourage me to assist. I would argue back in my own mind that I couldn't get to it because of the ditch. I started to get ideas of how it could work. I think the tree was smarter than I am because I swear it gave me some good ideas of how to get this done. There seemed to be some sense of urgency for the tree.

I invested in a few clippers and trimmed back the vines that were choking it. They were so angry with me that they got their revenge as best they could. Anyone who has cut down vines knows they take their revenge by whipping the face, cutting the skin and causing entanglements and falls. I wasn't able to clear very close to the maple because of the ditch it was situated in.

The tree told me to wait until snowfall. It "said" that the ice would create a surface that I could use to get close to it and finish the job. So one night when I wouldn't be seen, I took out my clippers and cleared away the rest of the vines as much as possible. In the spring, I moved back a log near the tree and pulled off the dead vines that the tree was once enmeshed in that now were hanging like rope off of it. I was satisfied that this tree could thrive and regain its health.

Spring came and the vines that held it down still dangled like ropes, but they were less and less prominent. It took until way into the summer to get its leaves back, but it did start to look normal, and I was happy that I helped. I thought that was the end of it.

Later that summer, I came back home after being away for a few days. I was shocked into an awareness of the maple tree's situation and why the tree was so emphatic that I help it when I did. The whole grove of trees that I communed with every day was gone! A stark, ugly low wall was exposed between properties. Yards of beautiful grass were ripped out and the ground was covered with tar. My friends, the trees, were ripped out by their very old roots to improve the large parking lot they were lining.

These trees had been magnificent and beautiful. They brought so much peace to the property. They provided nature and shade and a wonderful life force to an otherwise stark area. They were my comfort and my friends and every one of them was mowed down without a trace of any reverence for the fact that they were healthy and hundreds of years old. And now they were gone.

My heart was broken. My only solace was that at the end of what was a grove, there was one survivor. One tree was deemed worthy to exist by the men in yellow machines. My friend the maple tree now stands alone. It still has some vines dangling from it. But it made it! I don't think it would have without my help. And then I knew why it was so adamant that I help it when I did. I believe my friend knew its fate otherwise. The tree reaching out to me showed me that it has a sense of survival instinct and an eagerness to live.

And if my maple tree friend wanted to survive, I imagine the multiple billions of trees around the world that have known their fate, yet were destroyed, also wanted to survive. The loss and suffering is even more devastating than the human psyche can comprehend.

The Whisperings of a Balsam Fir

I was compelled to bring this little potted fir tree home with me recently. Once in a while, a plant in a store that is dying of thirst, light deficiency, or craving freedom will ask for me to rescue it. I do what I can. But this little tree was healthy and content.

It was part of a huge Christmas display at the local grocery store. It was in an entrance way that was swept up in the holiday spirit. I was also compelled to buy lights and special decorations for this little tree. I already had a big tree, so the strong pull to decorate this little tree was funny.

When I got the lights home, I started to realize that this tree was excited to be decorated. It wanted to have the Christmas tree experience. I put some lights on it and a couple of decorations, but it wanted more. It wanted the whole experience.

I had little bows that I could put on it, but I thought the cats would just pull them off and destroy its branches. The tree assured me they would not. He was right. My little rascals did not touch one bow or bulb on this little tree. They are very interested but very respectful.

I witnessed something that very few people are able to experience. This little tree told the cats not to harm it and they complied. They have destroyed favorite plants and other pines in the past. But this tree is beyond reproach. It let them know that it was off-limits.

This little tree is so joyful to have the Christmas tree experience and then get to go back into the ground in spring. It told me that all trees communicate with other trees through the roots. It was going to share the experience with all the other trees outside. They are perplexed with our practice of destroying them and giving them attention when they are dead but ignoring them when they are alive...the whisperings of a Balsam Fir.

This little tree is so excited to be celebrated in life. He says that many little trees would be happy to join in the celebration when they are young, and that that experience will stay with them all through their life. He tells me how much trees are happy to interact with people in their life. Every tree is a giving tree.

He is a bit overzealous. He wants his lights on all the time, but as insistent as he is, it is a respectful request. There is no feeling of being pulled or a sense of manipulation. It is as if love itself is speaking with me, and I believe it is.

Why a Compost

Animals and plants speak to us, and all of life will reveal its truth if we listen. Some people say that I am wise. I believe I am actually a very good listener. I think everyone can better tune into the things around them and become somewhat of a "Conscious Whisperer."

I have been given a profound truth from consciousness. I will share it because it is relevant to all. Recently, I have been collecting my peels from the pomegranates that I eat. I have collected a few and am reluctant to throw them out. I have always wanted a compost but am not in a position to have one. Yet, I am "told" by the life force in the peels that they want to be put back into the ground.

I have never been motivated by what is politically correct. Not that I don't agree with everything that is just and true in the world but because I don't want to be part of any group just for the sake of belonging to something. In fact, I may not do something that is good just because of the resistance of not wanting to be told what to do.

Having said that, I believe that composts are very good, not only for all the reasons that are already listed, but because the energies in our discarded organic waste want to be returned to the ground. It is a way to honor their service to us. Honoring a plant from the first time we put it in the ground to the time we lay it back into the ground is a way to honor ourselves and our own journey.

I would love to see all apartment complexes adopt composts as an option for all their tenants. I would love to see a compost service in all cities. It would be a matter of trucks hauling it away to huge compost lots that convert it into rich soil and then it could be sold or given away to enrich the foliage in local parks. Some industrious people could invest in a huge mixing truck and start their own little business by using it as a mobile composter. They could make income by hauling it away and selling it back out.

A compost pile is a sacred place. Organic items have consciousness. They want to return to the ground. They are grateful that you did that for them. That way, they can return to the earth and be whole. My friend and I know what items want because we listen to them. I have taught her and she is a master at it.

Many times she will tell me, "it wants to be returned to the ground." It is a sacred way to live: listening to those around it who are not speaking with their lips. It is the ultimate act of living in gratitude.

The Persona of Plants

Just because they don't scream or laugh in a way that our physical ears can hear doesn't mean that plants don't have consciousness. It is humans in their arrogance that invalidate other beings by their limited perception of them.

There is a symbiotic relationship between beta fish and bamboo. My bamboo was dying. It was a gift from someone who wanted to get rid of it. It was accepted half-heartedly. It was a few bamboo stalks tied together in a crisscross pattern. It just existed in this pattern for many months.

One day, I gave it some attention and snapped off all the wires that were holding it in place. I imagined each stalk as a person that was being unshackled from another person. It made the process of freeing them more poignant. I cleaned out its rotted roots, placed it in a bowl of water and felt the freedom and relief in the group of roots.

But still they continued to wilt. I got the nudge to add a beta fish to the bowl. I bought a bright red beta that seemed very pleased with his new home. Roscoe the Beta loves Ling-Ling the Bamboo. In my research on beta, it said that it was a fallacy that beta and bamboo gave each other a nutrient that the other needed. But seeing them, I knew that there was a benefit to them being together. The symbiotic nutrient is love and companionship. In a short time Ling-Ling the bamboo plant was rejuvenated.

I had already learned that plants feel emotions from an experience with my only other plant, Francis. I spend hours taking pictures of my dog and cats. One day, I decided that I should send a photo of Francis to the woman who gave him to me. He has grown very large very quickly. As I took the photo of him, I got the very distinct impression of pride. Francis was experiencing me taking the photos and felt pride that he was being included. It was a sacred moment that changed my relationship with all living things.

I was telling a friend on the phone about my new beta fish named Roscoe and his bowl mate, the bamboo. She asked me what the bamboo's name was. I hadn't thought of it but at that moment the vision of a famous panda popped into my head and I said that its name was Ling-Ling. My friend gasped in amazement because that was the name that just popped into her head, too. Did Ling-Ling the bamboo plant tell us both its name at the same time?

I think Roscoe and Ling-Ling know I am writing about them. They are pleased, but understand that we aren't going to change worldviews. We know the ramifications would be too unbearable for the human mind, as we hear a wood chipper outside.

Become a Plant Whisperer

I got a nudge to go into a wholesale supermarket one day. I sensed there was something there I was to pick up for a friend. Mentally, this seemed ridiculous because this friend doesn't eat processed foods. But I have learned to listen to my nudges. (A nudge is that nagging sense within to do something. It is a higher awareness nudging me closer to a higher conscious awareness.)

There was nothing that would appeal to her, but as I was leaving, I saw why I was there. There were beautiful orchid plants wrapped up in cellophane "dying" to be back in natural sunlight. I picked the first one I was drawn to for her and also got another one that was screaming for freedom. I could not put back the one that I had first chosen because I would feel bad leaving it behind. So I got both.

This situation happens often lately. I will be drawn into places not realizing why at first and then knowing it is to save the plants. A few weeks ago, there was a cactus in a drugstore that I rescued from the clearance aisle. I took it to a plant sanctuary for it to live out its days (my friend's house). The next time I saw it, it was sitting in the front window in a new pot emanating great pride. I saw how much it mattered.

Another time, there was a row of plants in a different supermarket that were bone dry. I can't take them all, so I pick out the ones that seem to need love the most or are thriving the hardest and adopt them as surrogates for the whole group. That day, I chose two plants and went up to the service desk a bit tongue in cheek. "I have a complaint," I said. "It isn't for me, but these plants have a complaint. They are very thirsty and have been neglected." (The plants in the cart loved the validation). The woman promised to have the rest watered.

I took them to my friend's house, and she poured her love into them. She named them, transplanted them, introduced them to the other plants and figured out which window they wanted to be in. The next time I visited, she was excited to show them to me. In less than a week, they more than doubled in size. Seriously. The love, validation and their gratitude were brimming out of their stalks.

Plants love just as much as people or animals do. It is we who have to tune our settings to be aware. It is we who are missing out on the love. Every blade of grass is screaming out with love if only we learn to acknowledge it.

So when I took the orchids to my friend's house, she looked stunned. She had just been in a home repair store and was drawn to the orchids there. As much as she wanted to get one, she denied herself and them. It was like the Universe had me step in to validate her worthiness to accept her bounty. My friend has recognized that partaking in the wonderment of life is like taking ourselves off the shelf.

A Jenuine Forest!

How many trees are in a forest? How close do the trees have to be to consider it a forest? Can they be spread out all over town, a country, or even the world?

I watch all these little saplings come up every year, and they have no chance of thriving in someone's flowerbed, but they still come up each year. Each one is a living example of optimism and potential. Why do we let them die so easily? Why do we put so little value on them? If they were humans, we would be creating a political agenda to protect their rights. But each tree perpetually gives. That is their nature. Not all humans contribute. For me, it is necessary to honor these trees and to value their infancy and to give them a safe place to plant their roots in the ground.

So I am starting a Jenuine Healing Forest. Please, if anyone local wants to adopt some saplings and commit to finding them a forever home in someone's yard or property, I would greatly appreciate it. If someone has some land and is willing to commit to taking some saplings, that would be wonderful. If there are any teachers who want to teach their children about the importance of trees and want to ask each child to find a home for a tree, that would be great! If there are any new parents out there, it is a wonderful gift for your children to have a tree that is the same age as they are.

When I was a child, I always wanted to do this. But maybe it was foreshadowing for this cause. Maybe the world needs it now. Let's start a movement. Let's create a forest! We can document where each tree is and have photos and inspire others to do the same. If you have saplings in your yard, maybe you can plant them and find them forever homes. It is a great way to give the love back to the trees.

Preserving the Moment

The old controlling factions, what we call "the powers that be," didn't want people to live long healthy lives. They preferred that they died younger because it is easier to control a mind from birth. Someone who is born into fracking, gmo's and gray air accepts it more readily. That is why it is important for us who are here to remain as healthy and unresponsive to power as possible.

In this way, truth has a chance to take hold once again. The generations that come will still be able to realize the beautiful expression of a tree and how it gives us its fruit. They will still be able to engage other species and learn more of humanity from them. They will also realize that a moment in nature is worth hours of being buried in synthetic materialism. What we have as blessings in this moment must be maintained, preserved and enhanced by us now.

The next generation must have the same imagery of beauty to glean from. It is here and now we take a stand. We empower ourselves in the moment. It has always been, and will always be, the moment.

A Mother's Love

There are a few maple saplings from last year that did not want to be mowed down. One in particular was pretty adamant in wanting to be left to grow. I definitely got the vibe from him that he wanted to grow to adulthood, but he wanted to secure his chances by telling my friend. When she walked down the driveway where he was growing, she turned to me and offhandedly said, "He wants to stay." It was as if it were the most natural thing in the world, which it is with us.

He was so proud when I mulched him. Someone ate his leaves so there was only a little stick in the center of a little pile of mulch. But he grew more leaves this year. Today, when I was watering the flowers, I made a point to water the little maples as well. What happened next was truly amazing. I got the distinct impression that the big tree that provided the seeds for the baby maples was satisfied in seeing the saplings get quenched.

It was further validation of what I have known. Trees love and nurture their children just like parents care for theirs. That feeling of wanting your children to thrive and be well-off, trees have this for their young as well. It is a revelation that has far reaching ramifications. Imagine the love and nurturing that is going on undetected by most humans. It is a shame that they don't benefit from recognizing the symbiotic relationship between parent and child in the tree genus. Maybe it would give more inspiration to humans to witness such a thing. I know it has enriched me.

A Surrogate for Nature

In the suburb of a large city, I see a lot of wildlife in my backyard. My house backs up to a glen so it is reasonable to fathom that. But I am amazed at the beautiful wildlife thriving in this suburb. Thank goodness they go unnoticed by most people lest they be labeled pests and "be dealt with." But for myself, I am grateful to know that such a plethora of deer, fox, coyote, possum, skunks, raccoon, gopher, hawks, chipmunks, bunnies, jackrabbits, squirrels and an array of birds are thriving.

On the news, it showed a property in my neighborhood that developers wanted to get their hands on. Many of these deals go through with the slick sales pitch and promises of abundance by the developers. They can't even fathom that nature unadorned and free is abundance. They just see something that they can slice up into little parcels and sell.

Developers don't see the genocide of whole ecosystems that are already living on the land that they are destroying. Just like the white man never acknowledged the genocide of great nations of Native Americans when crisscrossing ugly tracks all over America, so many people are still living with such a myopic linear limited outlook on life. They are the ones that wreak havoc on others in this world.

They don't acknowledge anything that isn't human as having value in terms of quality of life. They don't see the millions of homes in the humble ground that they will be destroying or all multitudes of families they will be ripping apart. They are impervious to their own acts of desecration.

A couple of years ago, I came home from a retreat and found a whole grove of very old trees chopped down and bulldozed out. The neighboring company wanted to extend their parking lot. That was all it took. Sure, there were meetings to stop it, but the deals were made. Later that day, the crows asked me why man had destroyed their homes? I had no answer. It is easier to understand crow than man.

On the news that same week, a man was crying in an interview.

His house had been destroyed in a flood. He was crying, "Why is God punishing us?" I had no compassion at all for him losing his home. None. God had not punished him. Man curses himself a million times over with the desecration that he continues to do to all species that don't look exactly like him.

He can only perceive the coarsest guttural sounds. Yet it is good to advocate for nature. The sweet soothing expressions of its gratitude make sharing this world with the ignorance of humans almost tolerable.

A Wonderful World

Life is communicating to everyone all the time through inner channels. The birds tell me what kind of seed they want, and the squirrels put in their order for more nuts in the food. The arbor vitae will wake me up in the middle of the night to shake the heavy snow off his limbs. He is proud to wear my scarf around him so that his limb doesn't separate from the main trunk.

The deer at my friend's house tell me that she is out of apples, so I show up at her door with some, so they don't have to miss one day of them. The trees in the neighbor's yard don't comprehend property lines so they wonder why they never get attention. It really is a wonderful world if we introduce ourselves to the wonder.

A Zen State of Being

A Technique from the Trees:

People open up their energy above them like a tree opens up its branches. But trees also open up their energy below them in the way they stretch out their roots. Both the branches and the roots arc around the body creating a protective orb of energy. The tree is still open and receptive but also protected in the orb of openness.

People do not do this. Since they usually don't open up and arc their energy below them, and only some people open up the energy above them, they remain in a vulnerable state. What they have learned to do is recoil or curl up in a protective ball. But this is not Joy, Love, Abundance, Freedom or Wholeness. It is a vulnerable state.

Imagine yourself as a mighty oak. They have the best analogy for deep, strong roots and great branches. Feel your energy dig deep into the Universe below your feet. Forget about the ground. For this purpose, the earth gets in the way as being too solid. Stretch out those roots and arc them open to slightly curl back up as a mirror to how branches curl down.

Now open up the energy above as if you were opening up your arms and even extending them more, like branches. Imagine the energy of the tips of what would be your branches extending to connect with the tips of the energy that would be your roots. See them coming together all around you until you are wrapped in this energetic orb of your own gratitude and openness. You are now open, yet contained, expansive and yet invulnerable. This is a Zen state of being.

A tree's heart chakra is in its trunk, a third of the way up.

Accepting One's Own Nature

(Say each statement three times out loud while CONTINUOUSLY tapping on the top of your head at the crown chakra and say it a fourth time while tapping on your heart Chakra. Pause before "in all moments.")

"I release complaining about the weather; in all moments."

"I release being disgruntled with life; in all moments."

"I release wasting energy on complaints; in all moments."

"I release fighting my own nature; in all moments."

"I release undermining Gaia; in all moments."

"I release cursing Gaia; in all moments."

"I release complaining about Gaia; in all moments."

"I release desecrating Gaia; in all moments."

"I release negating my own nature; in all moments."

"I release the disconnect between myself and Gaia; in all moments."

"I release the belief that I am separate from Gaia; in all moments."

"I release having discord within myself; in all moments."

"I accept Gaia as my nature; in all moments."

"I shift my paradigm to be in agreement with nature; in all moments."

"I am centered and empowered in my love and appreciation for Gaia; in all moments."

"I resonate and emanate love and appreciation for Gaia; in all moments."

Advice from a Tree

It's not your true nature to be so defined

By pettiness of emotions or feebleness of mind

You are more like the redwood, the mightiest of tree

Not creeping and needy like an intrusive vine

Stop clinging and clawing around the concept of great

Stand firm and erect as you claim your true fate

Pretending to be unworthy when you really know who you are

It's diminishing yourself that makes you irate

You know your own wonder but refuse to show it to others

So you fight amongst yourselves like a houseful of brothers

You cringe, and cower, recoil and hide

You only hint of your true self to yourself and your mother

This whole world of humans aren't where they should be

Each should be halfway to the sky if they were a tree

But they cover the ground like a new sapling crop

So vested in each other that they refuse to break free

They could have an amazing vantage point so high in the sky

They would be empowered and believe they could fly

All the while being grounded and rooted in earth

But they rescind their own greatness to just getting by

Fear of your own growth is the ultimate sin

It leaves you disfigured and unable to win

It seems quite overwhelming but growth is something you can do

Knowing your own nature is where you begin.

7/26/15

What the Sapling Forest Is Teaching Me About Healing

There are over three hundred little terracotta pots on my balcony. They all want me to give them individual attention. They thrive on it. Every day, I have to scan each one to see if they have enough sunlight, enough water and are feeling validated. It is important. It isn't enough to treat them as merely a whole unit and be done with it. They would all start to wither in groups.

It occurred to me that these little pots are kind of like all the cells in the body. They need individual attention to thrive and so do the cells of the body. Maybe there is a lot of healing in just giving all the cells in the body a nod of approval each day. Maybe it is a way of keeping them plugged in and feeling validated.

Each day in contemplation, scan the whole body very slowly and send love to each cell. Look at each one as if you were scanning a magnifying glass over it and enlarging it. See how they all feel and look. Start with the feet and make certain the cells of each toe and both heals get a quick look. Send all parts love.

Go through the whole body this way.

You may feel tingling, warmth or a magnetic sensation. It is the energy being stimulated in the body. It is evidence that what you are doing is effective. You may get tired or energized. Feeling the energy will affect people differently and will not always be consistent.

Scan your body this way every time you think of it. If you find lumpy energy, break it apart. If there are dark spots, pour light into them. You may surprise yourself with what you find and what you are capable of tending to. This is what a medical intuitive does, and you can do it for yourself. It is just one more opportunity for self-empowerment.

Advocate for Mother Earth

If Mother Earth were a person, she would be a nurturer and giver like so many of us. She would overlook people's faults to her own detriment. She would have to decide to self-regulate and take care of her own needs. These taps are done as a surrogate for her, so she can be empowered to stop being used and treated like a doormat.

(Say each statement three times while tapping on your head and say it a fourth time while tapping on your chest.)

"We declare ourselves surrogates for Mother Earth in doing these taps; in all moments."

"We release being infested with parasites; in all moments."

"We release being taken advantage of; in all moments."

"We release being benevolent to the takers; in all moments."

"We slap the hands of the takers; in all moments."

"We release being fracked; in all moments."

"We heal all the wounds that fracking has caused; in all moments."

"We refuse to be fracked; in all moments."

"We collapse and dissolve all power structures that frack us; in all moments."

"We withdraw all our benevolence from all those who frack us; in all moments."

"We withdraw all our benevolence from all those who take from us; in all moments."

"We release being poisoned; in all moments."

"We withdraw all benevolence to all those who poison us; in all moments."

"We neutralize all those who poison us; in all moments."

"We neutralize all the poisons that we have tolerated; in all moments."

"We remove all vivaxes between ourselves and all takers; in all moments."

"We remove all tentacles between ourselves and all takers; in all moments."

"We remove the claws of all takers from our beingness; in all moments."

"We remove all programming and conditioning that all takers have put on us; in all moments."

"We remove all engrams that the takers have put on us; in all moments."

"We strip all illusion off of all takers; in all moments."

"We remove all masks, walls, and armor from all takers; in all moments."

"We withdraw all our energy from all takers; in all moments."

"We send all energy matrices of takers into the Light; in all moments."

"We send all energy matrices of takers into the Sound; in all moments."

"We command all complex energy matrices of takers to be escorted into the Light and Sound by our guides; in all moments."

"We collapse and dissolve all the portals of the takers; in all moments."

"We extract all takers from our beingness; in all moments."

"We deny access to all takers; in all moments."

"We nullify all contracts with all takers; in all moments."

"We release all symbiotic relationships with all takers; in all moments."

"We recant all vows and agreements between ourselves and all takers; in all moments."

"We remove all curses between ourselves and all takers; in all moments."

"We remove all blessings between ourselves and all takers; in all moments."

"We sever all strings, cords, and wires between ourselves and all takers; in all moments."

"We dissolve all karmic ties between ourselves and all takers; in all moments."

"We remove ALL that all takers have put on us; in all moments."

"We take back ALL that all takers have taken from us; in all moments."

"We extract all takers from all 32 layers of our auric field; in all moments."

"We heal all 32 layers of our auric field; in all moments."

"We repair and fortify all layers of our Wei Chi; in all moments."

"We extract all takers from our Sound Frequency; in all moments."

"We extract all takers from our Light Emanation; in all moments."

"We shift our paradigm from all takers to the purity of our empowerment; in all moments."

"We transcend all takers; in all moments."

"We infuse purity and healing into our Sound Frequency; in all moments."

"We imbue purity and healing into our Light Emanation; in all moments."

"We infuse purity and healing into all 32 layers of our auric field; in all moments."

"We saturate our whole beingness with purity and healing; in all moments."

"We convert everything that is not pure into Divine Love; in all moments."

"We eliminate the first cause in regard to all takers; in all moments."

"We are centered and empowered in the purity of our own empowerment; in all moments."

"We resonate, emanate, and are interconnected with all life in the purity of our empowerment; in all moments."

An Exchange

Just like a good rain settles the dust on a dry day, a snowfall settles the negativity in the air. All those thought forms of shoulds, gossip, complaints, needs, must haves, must do's and judgments are all weighted down to the ground and recycled back into the earth. Maybe they is more waste that our trees take and recycle for us. Just as trees absorb the carbon dioxide and exchange it with oxygen, maybe they do this with more subtle energies, too.

The tradition of gathering around Christmas trees was begun as a form of gratitude and appreciation for their wisdom and contribution. It was a sacred ritual. The tradition has been bastardized to diminish them to a prop in the backdrop of our gluttonous exchanges.

One year, I was hell-bent on getting the perfect Christmas tree. I wanted to use it as a distraction from my own pain. I found a great tree that was covered with pinecones. We hacked it down with little regard. When I was home alone with it, it was so angry. Why did I not listen earlier? It was thriving in giving its seed to the world. I interrupted its purpose. It was almost too big to use as home decoration. It had almost made it through each season until I came along and chose it. It was a horrible feeling.

This year, I plan to get a potted tree to put in the house. It will be the best solution to the dilemma of wanting to have a tree while wanting to respect another being's existence. When picking out a tree to bring home, you may want to ask it what it wants. If you must have a live tree, at least make certain that it is in agreement with being there. It could actually add a dynamic to the ritual. Instead of looking for the perfect looking tree, look for the one that wants to come home with you and be an honorary member of the family.

The Wisdom of the Trees

Have you ever wanted to help someone with something that you are really good at, but they don't acknowledge your gifts? Have you watched them flounder and just wished that they would accept your help? This is how the trees feel. They just sit by and watch us struggle when they are so willing to help us. They have so much wisdom to share.

Awakening the Boundless Beauty

Everybody wants to be acknowledged for their gifts. When someone cuts the grass and you smell that sweet succor, it is the grass desperate to share its gifts. Most likely the person cutting the grass right then is not appreciating the grass itself. The fragrance is molecules of the grass collecting on your nose hairs and traveling up to your brain to share themselves with you. It seems they go out to everyone wishing for a little respect and appreciation.

So when you smell anything organic like grass, flowers or even the aroma of a tree, please acknowledge the interaction and the gift. Send a thank you back to the giver. They will receive the appreciation just as mechanically as you received the gift. There is so much love and beauty that goes unacknowledged. This is a way to start awakening the boundless beauty in life.

Create Nature Parks

Billionaires should buy up blocks of foreclosed homes that
have become dilapidated and create nature parks out of them.
Wouldn't that be a great way to revitalize cities by returning
part of the land and having the healing properties of nature?

Channeling Chive

When I moved into my new home, my ten year old great-
nephew came over to see the place. He loved it. His
grandmother and I showed him all the trees and what they
were feeling or saying. I introduced him to the trees and
showed him the herb garden. He really felt at home connecting
so deeply to the nature in my yard.

By the front door was a broken pot with something that looked
like grass growing in it. It had been left by the last tenants,
made it through the winter and was just sitting there. I hadn't
addressed it yet, partly because I didn't really know what it was.

When my nephew saw it, he became quite indignant. He
started lecturing his grandmother and me in a way that wasn't
normal for him. He was getting all heated up about this little
pot. "Just because it doesn't look like much doesn't mean it
doesn't matter." He kept going on and on.

It wasn't until later that I realized that he was being a
mouthpiece for the pot of chive. It had suffered all kinds of
indignity, and it was letting us know that it didn't appreciate it.
Soon after, I planted it amongst the herb garden, and it is
thriving very well now. It seems happy and feels vindicated.

A Rainstorm

Did you ever wonder why it feels so good before a rainstorm? A rainstorm, to the trees and plants, is like their Thanksgiving dinner. They are excited and reverent for the incoming bounty just as we are when a holiday is approaching for us. We are feeling their enthusiasm and "excitement." Everyone is joyful.

A Kiss

Did you know that flowers control when they send out their fragrance and it is their way of giving a kiss?

Do Plants Fall in Love?

I have an aquatic plant that outlived the fish in the bowl. It didn't grow. It didn't change. It just was a live plant that I used to filter my cat's water. They enjoyed drinking out of its vase, so it was feeling useful still. I decided to get some bamboo to create a filtered water dish for my dog. Bamboo is a harmless plant to cats and dogs.

One stalk was extra long. The cats kept pulling it out of the dog's water bowl as a toy. I spared it this humiliating experience by putting it into the vase with the other aquatic plant. There seemed to be an instant chemistry between them. They seemed to really enjoy each other. It was a very real sense that I got.

Both plants looked like they hadn't ever grown at all until they were united. Now they are both experiencing a growth spurt that looks like love. It is so amazing to see both of them shoot up at the same time. It can only be explained through love.

Do This Tap on Your Dog or Cat

(Say it three times wile tapping on their head and say a fourth time while tapping on their chest or back.)

"We send sustenance, warmth, nurturing and freedom to all doggies (or kitties) through _____ (fill in with pet's name); in all moments."

You can do this with pet birds and reptiles, but instead of actually tapping on their head, tap above it. You can even do it with your favorite plants or trees.

Do Trees Sleep?

I remember the first time I realized fish sleep; it was, "of course." I went out to mist the kids last night in the sapling forest and they were unresponsive. I got the distinct feeling that I waited too long after they called me and they were asleep. They usually like me to say goodnight to them. But last night, I think they were all asleep when I went out there. It was just like the moment I discovered that fish sleep. Of course.

Family

Do you think of the trees outside your house as members of the family? They do.

What Is Sacred?

Either everything is sacred or nothing is sacred. Only the limited mind picks and chooses. If you honor the sweetness of your child then you must honor that same sweetness in all children, of all ages, of all races, of all species and of all genres. Even the trees care for the perpetuation of their uniqueness through their seedlings. How can anyone turn their face away from that sacred reverence in others that is so vulnerable in themselves?

Even a Blade of Grass

I was sitting in the grass talking to a friend. Mindlessly, my hands pulled out a piece of grass and ripped it in little pieces. Suddenly, I perceived a little inquisitive voice asking, "What did you do that for?" The blade of grass was perplexed and slightly annoyed. I had no answer.

Exercise to Expand the Mind/Universe Connection

Ask questions within yourself that you could not possibly know the answer to.

An aspect of yourself will scan the Universe looking for the answer. This is one way to expand consciousness.

Here are my questions today:

Does the tree sapling hold the same wisdom as the mighty

seasoned tree, or does it accumulate wisdom from life experience? Does it have the potential to tap into greater wisdom beyond its years? If so, is it tapping into its own wisdom or a Universal wisdom? Is it encumbered by the lack of experience of its new body?

And, how is a tree sapling different or similar to a baby human?

Feeding Humanity with My Wildlife Dash and Dine

Today is such a special day of celebrating my liberation from being held by a psychopath nine years ago. When I was starving and forced to walk around the property with the captor, I had to look down because I wasn't allowed to look at him. I would see old deer bones and turtle shells that were gnawed on because the animals were so hungry. I felt a connection to them because I was that hungry, too. I understood.

So as a celebration today, my friend brought me over a beautiful flowering plant as a gift. It smelled so beautiful. I wonder how many people realize that flowers and plants can control emitting their scent and they do so to communicate love to us. The person at the store gave my friend the plant for free, and she thought it was meant as a gift to me from life to say thank you to me. It was a sweet gift.

To celebrate the day, I put out special foods in the wildlife "dash and dine" that is my backyard. One of the critters asked for corn on the cob. The whole corn has been a popular choice on the menu these days. But they told me that if it is on the cob they can carry it easily to their family and feed the babies. Here what was on the day's buffet:

- cracked corn
- whole corn
- corn on the cob
- kettle corn
- sunflower seeds
- pistachio/walnut/ peanut mix
- bird seed
- chicken thighs
- rotisserie chicken
- raw eggs
- carrots
- apples
- grapes

When I moved into my new home last year, I was worried about spending too much money on the yard. My spirit guides came through very adamantly that there was no such thing as spending too much energy of any kind on the yard.

They said that the ground is emaciated from so many people sending their prayers up to the sky instead of pouring them into the earth. They also said that one of the most spiritual acts you can perform is to garden. It is energy well spent (without pesticides of course), because feeding energy into the ground is a great way to feed humanity.

Friendship

The concept of friends is overrated. Anything that is so easily lost isn't worth the energy to keep. You may forget the people that seem to be so important to you at any given time. But you can't lose sight of your responsibility to yourself.

The concept of having lots of friends is an illusion meant to lock us in a limited state of consciousness. Who does not outgrow many of their high school buddies? Perhaps if people would assume everyone is their friend, they wouldn't be held hostage in toxic relationships.

Perhaps growth happens in the fluidity and randomness of many exchanges. Most of my best and loyal friends are trees.

Get Back to Nature

(Say each statement three times while tapping on your head, and say it a fourth time while tapping on your chest.)

"We balance our circadian rhythms; in all moments."

"We align with nature; in all moments."

"We blend and merge with nature; in all moments."

"All imbalances with nature are extracted; in all moments."

"We are centered and empowered in the splendor of nature; in all moments."

"We resonate, emanate and are interconnected with all life in the splendor of nature; in all moments."

Heal the Earth

(Say each statement three times while tapping on your head, and say it a fourth time while tapping on your chest.)

"All human superiority is released; in all moments."

"All fear and demonization of wildlife is released; in all moments."

"All synthetic barriers between wildlife and humans are removed; in all moments."

"All desecration of the ecosystem is repaired; in all moments."

"All ignorance of nature's wonder is removed; in all moments."

"All genocide of genres and species is stopped; in all moments."

"All self-righteousness targeting animals and nature is removed; in all moments."

"All fracking is immediately stopped; in all moments."

"All rights of citizenship are granted to all trees and species; in all moments."

This one can be said every day:

"The Earth is healed, all animals are honored, the wisdom of trees is revealed; in all moments."

Help Everyone Appreciate the Trees!

Here are the taps from the group session. The trees are really happy to have humans reconnect with them. These taps will help people see the value in trees, communicate with them and glean wisdom from them.

(Say each statement three times while tapping on your head and say it a fourth time while tapping on your chest.)

"We declare ourselves surrogates for trees in doing these taps; in all moments."

"We release being taken for granted; in all moments."

"We release being denied civil liberties; in all moments."

"We release being thought of as dead consciousness; in all moments."

"We release being disrespected; in all moments."

"We release being randomly killed; in all moments."

"We release being chopped up for parts; in all moments."

"We release being desecrated; in all moments."

"We release being targeted by the lust of man; in all moments."

"We release being sacrificed for silly rituals; in all moments."

"We release being the target of genocide; in all moments."

"We release having our wisdom ignored; in all moments."

"We release being disgraced by the ignorance of man; in all moments."

"We release being ignored by man for trying to save man from himself; in all moments."

"We dissipate all psychic energy that perpetuates ignorance in man; in all moments."

"We release being subjugated by the ignorance of man; in all moments."

"We release being sacrificed to the ignorance of man; in all moments."

"We release being killed off by the ignorance of man; in all moments."

"We release helplessly watching while the insanity permeates the earth; in all moments."

"We release reaching the point of no return; in all moments."

"We release trying to connect to man; in all moments."

"We release giving up on man; in all moments."

"We release shutting down; in all moments."

"We reawaken from our slumber; in all moments."

"We release having our love desecrated; in all moments."

"We remove all vivaxes between ourselves and the ignorance of man; in all moments."

"We remove all tentacles between ourselves and man; in all moments."

"We dissipate all the psychic energy that is the by-product of the ignorance of man; in all moments."

"We dissipate all the psychic energy that prevents man from communicating with us; in all moments."

"We remove all engrams of ignorance from man; in all moments."

"We remove all blind spots and denial from man; in all moments."

"We remove all programming and conditioning to be ignorant from man; in all moments."

"We awaken the subtle senses of man; in all moments."

"We release the lasciviousness of man; in all moments."

"We remove all root rot caused by man; in all moments."

"We send all energy matrices into the Light and Sound that cause man to be ignorant; in all moments."

"We command all complex energy matrices that cause man to be ignorant to be escorted into the Light and Sound; in all moments."

"We release being inundated by the ignorance of man; in all moments."

"We release being taken out of our joy by the ignorance of man; in all moments."

"We release being taken down by the selfishness of man; in all moments."

"We nullify all contracts with the ignorance of man; in all moments."

"We release being let down by man; in all moments."

"We release being abandoned by man; in all moments."

"We release resonating with the ignorance of man; in all moments."

"We release emanating with the ignorance of man; in all moments."

"We extract all the ignorance of man from our Sound frequency; in all moments."

"We extract all the ignorance of man from our Light emanation; in all moments."

"We dissipate all the ignorance of man; in all moments."

"We transcend the ignorance of man; in all moments."

"We empower man to transcend ignorance; in all moments."

"We protect ourselves from being violated by man; in all moments."

"We make space in this world to thrive and propagate; in all moments."

"We remove all blockages in this world to thriving and propagating; in all moments."

"We stretch our capacity to thrive and propagate in this world; in all moments."

"We make space in this world to reconnect with all humans; in all moments."

"We remove all blockages to reconnecting with all humans; in all moments."

"We stretch our capacity in this world to reconnect with all humans; in all moments."

"We imbue all humans with our wisdom; in all moments."

"We imbue all humans with a sense of their transgressions against us; in all moments."

"We instill peace in all humans; in all moments."

"We release being demonized by humans; in all moments."

"We instill respect for us in all humans; in all moments."

"We resonate, emanate, and interconnect with all humans in higher consciousness; in all moments."

How to Create a Love Grid

A message from the Lemurian crystals:

You know that old game of taking two tin cans, poking a hole in the bottom, tying a string between them and making a makeshift telephone? If you talk into one can, someone else can hear what you say through the stretched out string by listening into the other can. It works because sound frequencies are carried on the string.

The crystals tell me, in a similar way, that they are connected to all other crystals. We can create a love grid by keeping a Lemurian crystal with us and pouring love into it. Give a Lemurian crystal to everyone you love and you will stay connected to them in the love. It is like having love walky-talkies. Everyone who has a crystal will be connected in the love to everyone else who has a crystal.

It is a great way to feed love into this world and to feed love, awareness, and positive and healing energy to all those who love. I have a Lemurian crystal that is with me constantly so we will be connected in the love.

A Tree's Observation

I asked my sapling forest and the big trees to tell me one of their secrets. They showed me in images how silly man is by chopping up existence into different outfits. They showed me a man mowing his lawn in boxers and a tee, and they showed me a man in a power suit. They think it is silly how the different outfits change the whole feeling of the man. They believe it is the outfits that are creating the mood. Maybe they are right.

Experiencing the Devastation of the Tree

I have always loved Dolly Parton. She has come from humble beginnings and never lost her humility. She has stayed true to herself, her music and her southern roots. When I was a child, I remember her winning an award and, as her name was announced, her dress split open.

With the grace and likeability of a genuine person, she went up to receive her award with a shawl or something covering herself. She then said something that was so charming and real that it made her all the more endearing. She said something to the effect of, "Well my grandmamma always said that's what happens when you put 20 pounds of potatoes in a 10 pound sack." Delightful.

I was sad to see that she was going to be a guest at the lighting of the Christmas tree celebration at Rockefeller Plaza. It was sad to see any celebrities there, but especially her because she has such appeal and love for the backwoods of Tennessee. For the last couple of years, these marvelous, hundreds of year old trees that are slated to be cut down as Christmas trees and displayed at Rockefeller Plaza have communicated with me to help save them from this fate.

They want to live and continue their loving beautiful purpose. But I have too small a voice in the world of greed and power to prevent their demise. It has brought excruciating pain to me to feel the helplessness and the loss of such wisdom and beauty on this planet.

On a seemingly unrelated topic, it was recently reported that Dolly Parton was devastated that her labor of love, Dollywood, was destroyed due to forest fires. This came to fruition around the same time as the airing of the lighting of the Christmas tree at Rockefeller Plaza. They weren't unrelated to me.

I can perceive in energy how devastated the Christmas tree was to be killed for such a frivolous purpose. I can perceive in energy how devastated Dolly Parton is to lose her namesake theme park. They are pretty much equal in devastation. People will argue that the theme park brought jobs and joy to so many. Advocates of the tree would explain that the tree brought life sustaining oxygen and as much joy to the planet as the theme park did. The two events are directly related.

This is how karma works. Dolly Parton is not being punished for her lack of understanding of the depth of a tree's awareness. Her celebrating the death of this tree is beneath her level of goodness, but she is getting an equal amount of pain and loss as the tree received. This is how compassion is sown and harvested. Miss Parton may never directly connect the two experiences unless perhaps she stumbles upon this article, but she is ever changed by the events that have occurred to quicken her process of awakening to more of life's wonders.

Perhaps next year, the producers of this lighting of the tree event will ask her to come back again. Perhaps she will associate it with the devastation of her lovechild and decline. This is how compassion and awareness spread. It is not always done with an epiphany and a shaft of light breaking through the heavens. It is done in a peripheral way that may be more painstaking to endure but is still ingrained in the chronicles of our existence. Perhaps you can see your own coincidences in these words. Maybe it will save some wear and tear on your emotions along the way.

Written by a Tree

Open up the floodgates

Between the human and Divine

Rest yourself in sweat stained sheets

Let your ego lay supine

Offer yourself up to the heavens

That beckon you to undress

The real self walks in brilliant wonders

That the mind cannot suppress

Bring a gift back to this world

A memory or insight

Leave it as a "bread crumb trail"

So others may take flight.

4/21/14

Adopt a Tree

If you are struggling to realize your self-worth, may I suggest adopting a tree? Trees are great for reflecting the serenity of our depth to us so we can embrace our own omniscience beyond the pettiness of the ego. If you ever have any kind of creativity block, go outside to a tree that catches your fancy and create, in the venue you are comfortable with, while under the tree. You will be surprised that all the resistance will melt away. Trees are the best poets!

Keeping Humanity Alive

Everyone but humans

See roads as just their land

The real danger they accost

Only humans understand

People are the only ones

That dismiss the worth of trees

To all others they are a safe way

Neighbors, lodging, food, communities

Humans are the only ones

Who dismiss the plight of others

Every other specie lives in harmony

They see all life as brothers

Humans are the only ones
Who destroy life just for fun
Others find it a necessity
It's been this since life's begun

Humans are the only ones
Who desecrate the land
They do it out of ignorance
And just because they can

Humans are the only ones
Who overemphasize their worth
They've been taught to magnify their importance
Ever since their birth

But trees, fresh water, bugs, plants and animals
Exist more than to help humans survive
They are the real heroes of this world
They keep humanity alive.

The Rescue

Last night, outside of my routine, I emptied the garbage at night. In the dumpster were two half-dead lily plants. I am ashamed to say I was torn between whether I should bother with them or not. I brought them in the house and put them in the sink to water them. I gave them a shower. They popped back to life within minutes. It took so little. Their presence just filled my home. They were grateful and a strong vibrant energy. I wondered if they called to me from the house.

I put them in the bedroom so the cats couldn't eat them. When I went back down the hall, I got a creepy sensation that someone was in my house. Oh, yes, it was the lilies. They were invited guests. My friend graciously agreed to have them come live at her house. She came the next morning to pick them up. I had a strong nudge to go check out the dumpster. Buried under all the bags was another plant. It made it through the night. I wouldn't have been able to get it then, but it called to me this morning. It will be fine, too.

The ability to listen affords many adventures and surprises that life brings through paying attention. Sure some may say, "What is the big deal? It is only a plant." I cannot even explain to them the joy that comes from not valuing people over other life forms. It puts that childlike wonder back into life. It gives the direct awareness that life is not about having. Life is about being: Being engaged, being of service, being joyful!

Please, if you see any living thing discarded, do yourself a favor and rescue it. You will be rescuing yourself using it as a conduit.

Making Love

I went out to lay in the hammock like I do everyday. It is under the huge apple tree that is the focal point for the bird feeder and the deer to graze under. The tree is really happy with the communion that goes on within and around him. He is appreciative that I feed everyone under him.

When I went out there today, there was a perfect red apple in the hammock. It had no wormholes and was a pretty good size. It didn't fall through the netting of the hammock. I knew instantly that it was a gift from the apple tree to me.

As I lay in the hammock, I thanked the tree for his gift. He implied that there was a selfish motive. Selfish is the wrong term in describing a tree. But he told me more.

He told me that he wanted me to eat the apple so that he could experience the world through my consciousness. He explained that is the beauty of nature and how they share consciousness through ingesting each other. He showed me that when grass is eaten by rabbits and deer, they blend consciousness. And when the rabbit or deer is eaten in nature, they share consciousness through the being that ate them. In this way, all nature blends and is one.

He explained that humans are the only ones who separate themselves from this process. They do so by their compartmentalizing life and death and their handicap of linear thinking. He said that the only time humans get close to the process that nature is imbued in is in the heights of making love. Not sex, but love. He made this distinction.

He was teaching me to be conscious when I ingested the apple he gave me. In doing so, I would be shown the miracle of nature that is experienced a trillion times over, every day. There is no pain or sense of loss. There is only a transformation of form and an exchange of energy. It gave me an extended understanding of what other trees have told me in other learning sessions.

The apple was a very good gift.

One Note

I am a new person each moment

The one I am at the core

I am more free, lighter and happier

Than I was just a moment before

I can sing my own praises

I can dance in the mist or the rain

I can embrace every tragedy

As it teaches me to let go of the pain

I can actually swim with the fishes

Even if it's in my own mind

I commune with the dolphins, whales and the seals

As I leave all illusion behind

I continuously consult with my mentors

The long-standing wisdom of trees

They tell me the truth that men no longer speak

They send it to me on the breeze

I can withstand almost anything

Loss, loneliness, the plight of our youth

But I can't wear the lies of this world

I no longer will bury my truth

Which is...

You are a mystery waiting to reveal

You are the answer you seek

Open yourself up and just look inside

Whatever you tell you, just speak

Sing it to all who will listen

Knowing much will fall on a deaf ear

But it is so worth the performance

If even one note reaches someone to hear

3/28/16

Open Letter to Mayor de Blasio

Dear Mayor De Blasio,

I understand that you are very busy running the largest and most diverse city in the world. I would not bother you unless it were something that is very pressing. In your great city, everyone is so busy, personal space is congested and the ability to connect to nature is very limited. In fact, to many in your world, the connection with nature may seem as convoluted as unicorns and as frivolous as daisies. But I assure you it is not.

There is a practice in New York City that has become archaic. It may have been charming in a more simple time. It moved into indulgent a while back, and now it simply sends the wrong message to the world. Cutting down a 300 year old tree for a yearly celebration now has come to represent gluttony and indifference to those who are conscious of the world's needs. To those of an even more heightened awareness of the fine balance between society and nature, it is perceived as murder.

On a purely practical note, trees absorb carbon dioxide and release oxygen into the atmosphere which all of life depends on.

Trees are not dead plankton on the beach. They are living, breathing examples of wisdom and service. They literally provide the breath that we need to survive. Cutting down these creators of our life force sends a message of stagnant awareness and slavery to mass consuming. Certainly, it is wonderful to observe a 300 year old tree being lit up, but not if it is desecrated in the process.

There are many alternatives to killing a living being that is older than many generations. Perhaps a beautiful sculpture of a tree could be created that could be lit up each year. Perhaps a place should be reserved for a living tree to be potted. Each year people could delight at its yearly growth. It could be a perpetual mascot to the season. It would be more impressive than knowing that a dynamic tree is going to the wood chipper after the holiday sales.

I know you to be a man of integrity. I know you want to do the right thing. Please use your time on this earth to make a change that really will benefit all of humanity. You are in a position to send a very powerful message to the world that addresses global warming, pollution and the importance of trees. Please consider taking a courageous stance in this matter. Please stop the cutting down of an ancient tree merely to enhance the ambiance of consumers in December.

Thank you so much.

- Jen Ward

Pouring Abundance into the Ground

I was feeling guilty about wanting to buy some extras for my garden. My Spirit Guides intervened. They told me it is never a waste to pour love into the ground. Spending money on garden materials is a form of pouring love and abundance into the ground. It is never wrong to do so and the more the better.

The only exception would be using your abundance to endorse killing things. This includes poisonous mulch, pest control or weed killer. But to use your abundance to pour love in the ground is a great act of altruism. When you beautify your yard, you are pouring love into the earth. This love seeps all the way through the planet and uplifts all of life.

Update on the Sapling Forest

Many of the forest didn't make it after the move. They were fine up until then which was strange. They told my friend that they had come here to do what they needed to do. I know now that they gave me the incentive to get to my own home which motivated me more than my own means could do. There were only about 25 trees that remained. They are mostly cherry and walnut trees. It was just enough that the grounds out back can support.

They wanted to go in the ground during the strawberry harvest moon last night. There was some significance to that time because it was also the day I was compelled to adopt 20 cactus plants. It was also the day that my friend, who had a huge crock of lilies that told her they wanted to be here with me, brought them over. It was a busy day.

There was another significance, too. I was not able to facilitate my group session last night. The phone could not understand my call-in number that I tried over 30 times and have been using fine for the last two months. I was blocked from doing so.

When my friend and I went to prepare the ground to receive the trees, it was crazy how easily the groundcover pulled away. It was almost effortless. It was like the covering knew it was temporary and just pulled itself up with no remorse. It's as if it realized that I don't like to interfere with anything that is living, and it did not want to create a moral conflict in me, or that everything was in agreement with and assisting the trees being planted.

The trees told my friend where they wanted to be. She is great at listening to them and giving me a second set of "ears," so I do what they wish. It is very convenient. They were so happy to get in the ground. They stood proud and happy. They wanted mulch around them so they wouldn't get lost in the ground covering.

An interesting thing happened. As we planted them into the ground, they were there physically, yet they disappeared energetically into the earth. It was hard to decipher their presence. It is as if they went to visit all their old friends through the rooting system and were only present in body. It was very strange. It left me sad because as we planted them, I couldn't find them.

They told me that they are just busy visiting all that they missed in being in the pots. We as humans think so much of us is about the physical form, but to them, and most likely us, the physical form is just an anchor for their consciousness in this world. They want me to be able to connect with them. They have told me to put a little border around each one of them, and when I physically look at them as individuals, it is like calling them to me. Otherwise, their consciousness will be wandering through the rooting system of the earth. They say this is how it is with trees. That is why addressing them individually is so important and why so many people miss out on that connection with trees. If you don't acknowledge them as individuals, they are only there in physical form.

They want this connection with me, but they are truly enjoying being back in the ground as well. It is such a peaceful feeling to sit amongst them. I feel they are the healers I believed them to be. Today, I will put the remaining ones into the ground and mark them all with rocks and mulch. They are so happy to have the best of both worlds. They are happy to have a connection with you and me through me, and to be free to connect with the earth again. Thank you all for your interest and please feel the love.

Message from the Trees

There will be a global shift when individuals wake up to their own power and start valuing integrity and kindness more than money and a show of force. A shift will occur when everyone simultaneously wakes up in their daily life. When they decide it is not worth it to fight with others, and it is not worth it to jump through hoops to be accepted. It is not worth it to listen to authorities as they run natural resources and organic living into the ground.

The reason believing in reincarnation is difficult is because it is acknowledging all the times we have suffered at the hands of power. Reincarnation is a means to remember all the deaths in war and giving our allegiance to unworthy convictions. It is devastating to be wrong, and to realize the plight of many lifetimes can be overwhelming. It is why there is so much depression in the world. There is such a heavy glass ceiling on all in general.

The answer is to listen to your own inner council. Turn off the voice of experts in your head. Lead by example instead of being an example of being led. Those who respect you will find their own strength, courage and allegiance to true justice. Reclaim your allegiance.

Once we collectively accept that power and control have a limited bag of tricks, we will all transcend from habitually falling prey to the tactics. We will celebrate freedom together.

Powerful Healing Technique to Benefit Every Tree

(Say each statement three times out loud while tapping on the top of your head at the crown chakra and say it a fourth time while tapping on your chest at the heart chakra.)

"I declare myself a surrogate for trees everywhere in doing these taps; in all moments."

"I release being stripped of my dignity; in all moments."

"I release being desecrated; in all moments."

"I release being raped of my essence; in all moments."

"I release being ignored; in all moments."

"I release having genocide committed upon me; in all moments."

"I release being randomly murdered; in all moments."

"I release being gleefully cut down; in all moments."

"I release having my wisdom ignored; in all moments."

"I release being at the mercy of ignorance; in all moments."

"I remove all vivaxes between myself and ignorant humans; in all moments."

"I strip all the illusion off of humans that makes them indifferent to me; in all moments."

"I release being at the mercy of ignorant humans; in all moments."

"I release being ripped from my home by ignorant humans; in all moments."

"I remove all tentacles between myself and all ignorant

humans; in all moments."

"I release the systemic abuse I've sustained at the hands of ignorant humans; in all moments."

"I make space in this world for every tree to be respected by all humans; in all moments."

"I remove all blockages to every tree being respected by all humans; in all moments."

"I stretch the capacity for every tree to be respected by humans; in all moments."

"I remove all programming and conditioning that ignorant humans have put on me; in all moments."

"I remove all engrams that ignorant humans have put on me; in all moments."

"I send all energy matrices into the light that immerse humans in ignorance; in all moments."

"I command all complex energy matrices that immerse humans in ignorance to be escorted into the light and sound by my guides; in all moments."

"I send all energy matrices into the light and sound that cause humans to defile trees; in all moments."

"I command all complex energy matrices that cause humans to defile trees to be escorted into the light and sound by my guides; in all moments."

"I nullify all contracts that ignorant humans have made with trees; in all moments."

"I remove all curses that ignorant humans have put on trees; in all moments."

"I recant all vows and agreements between trees and ignorant humans; in all moments."

"I remove all blessings between trees and ignorant humans; in all moments."

"I remove all ritualistic behavior that humans indulge in with regard to trees; in all moments."

"I sever all strings and cords between myself and all ignorant humans; in all moments."

"I dissolve all karmic ties between myself and all ignorant humans; in all moments."

"I send all energy matrices into the light that deduce humans to being brutes; in all moments."

"I command all complex energy matrices that deduce humans to being brutes to be escorted into the light and sound by my guides; in all moments."

"I lift the balm of ignorance from the land; in all moments."

"I collapse and dissolve all ignorance; in all moments."

"I release humans from resonating with ignorance; in all moments."

"I release humans from emanating with ignorance; in all moments."

"I extract all ignorance from the sound frequency of all humans; in all moments."

"I extract all ignorance from the light emanation of all humans; in all moments."

"I extract all ignorance from the whole beingness of all humans; in all moments."

"I extract all ignorance from the universal sound frequency of humanity; in all moments."

"I extract all ignorance from the universal light emanation of humanity; in all moments."

"I connect with all loving humans in the loving grid of acceptedness; in all moments."

"We are centered and empowered in loving communication with all humans; in all moments."

"I am centered and empowered in loving interconnectedness with all humans; in all moments."

Technique for Opening Your Heart and Shifting Your Reality

When driving down the road, acknowledge every tree that you pass by. See it as a sentient being that is greeting you as you pass because it is. You may even start to imagine them bowing with respect to you as you pass. They will be acknowledging you for acknowledging them when so many don't. See if this does not change the caliber of your drive, maybe even your life.

Technique to See Trees Dance

You can love everyone and everything all at once. You can be with them even though they are millions of miles away. The feelings of loss are an engram from past lives when you lost everything dear to you. It is not the case now. All of life is your friend and you are more in touch with love than ever before. Living and having experiences is not something to break your heart, no matter what the limited mind may say.

When we have experiences that cause us to feel deeply, no matter what the feeling, it is an invitation to awaken to more and more of the love and interconnectedness that is availed to us. It is not possible to lose anything. It is only the illusion of separation. And at this point in our evolution as a species, it is time to say good riddance.

Everything we think, say and do has been stripped down to the most limiting factor. We have been deduced to "stick figure" mentalities. It is so difficult to convey to stick figures in stick figure language that they are actually robust, effervescent exponential energy that is turning and churning upon itself like the dynamic properties of the very stick figure sun.

We are living in a "check the box" world where you are only afforded limited choices to identify with. Are you happy or sad, good or bad, pretty or unattractive, male or female? Why can you not be an intricate higher dimensional mosaic of all these things woven together and dancing within your atoms? Why does everything need to be so flat and lifeless in this world? I assure you it is not.

For example, when you look at a tree, you are never actually seeing that tree. Your mind has filtered out all the movement and dance that it is perpetually engaged in. Your stick figure mind has filtered it out. A tree is not rigid. A tree is not lifeless. Thinking and believing that is the stick figure mind inflicting its limitation on that tree. A tree, along with all life, is fluid, dancing, ecstatic, loving energy.

Try this technique: When you are in a grateful receptive "heart," place yourself in a comfortable place where you can observe a tree. Make it a special tree, one that you have affection for. Spend as long as it takes to just observe the tree. Ask it silently to show you its true self. Be receptive to taking off the filters of the eyes and mind that limit your perceptions. Look for movement in the tree's branches.

If your energy is receptive, you will see the tree undulating in an incredible powerful expression of life. You will see these huge limbs moving like arms and you will see it surge with movement and dance. Those who read my posts are aware of the energy of them. So know that the ability to see trees like this is infused as a gift in these words to you. I am gifting you with seeing as I see. The trees will be helping, too. These both, matched by your sincere intention, may afford you the ability to do this.

Meditation is used for getting out of body. But what is the point if you are going to ignore all the beauty that is around you where you stand? Or do you stand at all? Once you can see the tree move, you can look at neighboring trees and see them move as well. It is not they that are changed. It is you. You have taken off limiting filters on your mind. So meditation is not meant as an escape "out of here." It is a means to awakening to reality that you don't have to go anywhere to be everywhere.

The reason Van Gogh's painting of "Starry Night" is so profound is because he was seeing without the filters that others are equipped with. For him, it was insanity to see such beauty and experience life so exponentially while trying to live "normally" in a stick figure world. These are exciting times now. We are able to experience the expansiveness of consciousness while incorporating it into the limiting existence that has been agreed upon by mainstream.

It is time to change that agreement. By removing the limiting filters of a stick figure world, you will be infusing this present reality with much depth and joy. All you have to do is awaken yourself more and more and that will be infused into the collective agreement of humanity.

Fighting Injustice

Yesterday I went to the floral shop in my favorite local grocery store. I wanted to buy two single flowers. The woman in charge had subtle contempt for me right away. She refused. I told her I had bought flowers there before and since there was a witness in the form of another worker there, she agreed. I picked out two beautiful creamy orange roses that literally spoke to me. They were so lovely. Did you know that flowers send us love by emitting their fragrance? That is sort of their way of giving a hug. These flowers were hugging me.

She plucked the two of them out of the bucket and said, "I can't sell you those." She then proceeded to throw them on the top of the garbage. She said that these two perfect flowers were dying. I protested, but she would not rescind her position. The two perfect flowers that were emitting such love were lying on top of the garbage heap and there was nothing I could do about it.

My heart was aching. I wanted to save them. I even picked them up to smell them. They were so fragrant. I wanted to explain to her that their life was valuable to me. I wanted to explain that outer beauty was not the only criteria in choosing those two roses. I wanted to take these flowers home and honor their place in the world. I wanted to rescue them from being desecrated. It seemed that this woman had just thrown them away to display power over me. It was my fault they were in the trash. This was a subtle but huge injustice to me.

Of course, to say any of this would have made me look unbalanced. It didn't help that the other worker explained the mulching process in detail and how the two beautiful flowers were going to be ground up. I sat there in silence and took it. I failed those flowers. With all the injustice in the world, I realized that my silence and lack of ability to make these people understand the horrific act they were committing was my failing. What was worse, their ignorance or my silence?

I failed. I chose conforming instead of speaking my truth. I realize others would do the same thing, but maybe that is the problem. In contemplation, I was given an answer about the controversy over sharing horrific images to fight a cause or not. The answer I received was this: People have opportunities every single day to speak and defend their truth. If they don't do it in the small, subtle ways that the Universe presents to them - ways where they can truly be effective - then why bother trying to be effective in a grander way?

Truth is won everyday when we live in complete integrity and honor all life around us to the best of our ability. This is how we elicit change and uplift humanity. The place we do this is in our own home, work place and community. If we are complacent to truth in our daily lives, it is hypocrisy to expect the world to live in truth.

Releasing the Fear of Death

The fear of death only happens in humans because they are the only species that thinks linearly and is separated from others by its self-induced time line. With all other species, life rolls into itself. It blends and blurs and changes form through the process of love and ingestion of other forms of life.

The life cycles that we fear and avoid and inflict upon others as death and separation, other species welcome and embrace in love and interconnection. Not a warm fuzzy love but a mutual respect. Man is the only species that consciously hates. Perhaps man's pets, too, because they pick that up from man.

Other species may have a primal urge to avoid another species or even attack and kill. But it is never done in hate. It is part of a beautiful, cohesive cyclical process. That's why the topic of vegetarian or carnivorous does not happen in nature.

When a plant or animal is eaten in nature, its consciousness blends with the host who ingested it. It gains awareness from a new vantage point. This is because of the prevalent unspoken code of love that nature operates under and which humans are mostly devoid of.

The only way something can really be killed is if its consciousness is invalidated or disrespected at its transformation. This indifference is the real issue in the debate over vegan or carnivorous. There is just as much lack of appreciation of plant life as there is animal life. So people need not try to raise the awareness of a certain cause. They would serve humanity better in raising awareness in general.

Return the Sacredness of Water to the World

(Say each statement three times while tapping on your head and say it a fourth time while tapping on your chest.)

"I declare myself a surrogate for the world in doing these taps; in all moments."

"All water pollution is eliminated; in all moments."

"All desecration of sacred water is eliminated; in all moments."

"All enslavement to polluting sacred water is released; in all moments."

"All illusion is stripped off of water polluters; in all moments."

"All vivaxes with water pollution are removed; in all moments."

"All karmic imbalances with sacred water are eliminated; in all moments."

"All desperation due to water pollution is eradicated; in all moments."

"All apathy and indifference towards water pollution is removed; in all moments."

"All urge to disengage from caring about our sacred water is removed; in all moments."

"The poisoning of our sacred water is eliminated; in all moments."

"All masks, walls, and armor on all those who pollute our sacred water are removed; in all moments."

"All minimizing of the importance of our sacred water is removed; in all moments."

"All psychic attacks by those who cause water pollution are dissipated; in all moments."

"Desecration of sacred water is untangled from mass consciousness; in all moments."

"Desecration of sacred water is stripped away from mass consciousness; in all moments."

"All poisoning due to the desecration of sacred water is eliminated; in all moments."

"All tentacles with those that poison sacred water are severed; in all moments."

"All programming and conditioning due to water pollution are removed; in all moments."

"All engrams of desecration of sacred water are removed; in all moments."

"All energy and support for those who cause water pollution is withdrawn; in all moments."

"All muscle memory of water pollution is released; in all moments."

"All energy matrixes that allow sacred water to be polluted are sent into the Light and Sound to dissolve; in all moments."

"All complex energy matrixes that allow sacred water to be polluted are dissolved into the Light and Sound; in all moments."

"All contracts with water pollution are nullified; in all moments."

"All vows and agreements with those that pollute sacred water are recanted; in all moments."

"All curses of water pollution are removed; in all moments."

"All blessings of water pollution are removed; in all moments."

"All strings, cords and ties with water pollution are severed; in all moments."

"All karmic ties with water pollution are dissolved; in all moments."

"All energy is withdrawn from those who pollute sacred water; in all moments."

"All pain, burden and limitations of water pollution is removed; in all moments."

"All fear, futility and unworthiness that water pollution causes is removed; in all moments."

"All loyalty to those who pollute sacred water is removed; in all moments."

"All anger, entitlement and illusion of separateness induced by water pollution is removed; in all moments."

"All resonating and emanating with water pollution is released; in all moments."

"All lack caused by water pollution is removed; in all moments."

"All disease caused by water pollution is removed; in all moments."

"All that those who poison sacred water have taken is returned; in all moments."

"All wounds inflicted by water pollution are healed; in all moments."

"All desecration of sacred water is collapsed and dissolved; in all moments."

"All energy systems that have been compromised by water pollution are healed and repaired; in all moments."

"The sanctity of sacred water is restored; in all moments."

"All water of the planet is centered and empowered in purity; in all moments."

"All water of the planet is perpetually purified and honored with gratitude; in all moments."

"All water of the planet resonates, emanates and is interconnected with all life in purity; in all moments."

"All water of the planet is returned to purity; in all moments."

"All water of the planet resonates, emanates, and is interconnected with all life in gratitude and respect for its gift to the world; in all moments."

Update on the Forest

The trees that did thrive after the move wanted to be put in the ground on June 2. They were specific. It was a full moon. The trees that didn't make it wanted their terracotta pots broken up and put in the ground with the others. They said they held their essence in the pots and wanted to rejoin the others and be spirited in them. So it is a huge forest even though there are only a few trees.

Since then, it has rained almost everyday. They are thriving.

They are growing out of their baby bodies and starting to have the confidence of trees. They are very happy and wish me to go out and admire them daily. They send all their love and exuberance to every one of you.

They love being in the ground and when I planted them, they seemed to disappear from me. They told me that they just sunk into the earth to revisit old friends. They told me that the reason trees seem so lifeless to some people is that if they aren't being engaged, they will just sink their energy into the ground; their tree body is merely an outpost.

They explained that people are like this too but don't realize it as much. You know when you try to talk to someone who is engaged in something else, they seem a million miles away. That is because they are. They only come back to the body when they are addressed.

The saplings told me that they aren't really assigned an identity unless they are noticed in some way and stand out. All the saplings in the little forest I have started would have melted into the ground and discontinued to exist. But because I put attention on them and made space for them in this world, now they are individualized. They will grow to be mighty trees and share their gifts. They have a place and purpose in this world.

They told me the same thing is true with people. People are like little saplings in that they don't really reach their potential. They exist like little saplings unless someone notices the possibilities of their greatness and acknowledges them. When the potential of a person's greatness is recognized and highlighted, there is space made in this world for it. They can then accomplish great things.

The saplings say that there are not many people who exist beyond their sapling selves. But they said that is what my work is and does. I see and acknowledge the genius in all and hold a space for it to manifest, just as I hold space for more trees in the world. Both visions are important.

They say trees and people are not that different except trees know their nature and understand who they are as energy beings.

S.O.S! Please Help Save the Trees!

Everyone can do the exercise below as a way to make a dent in the thick consciousness of stubbornness and ignorance that have impersonated truth for way too long.

(Say each statement three times out loud while continuously tapping on the top of your head at the crown chakra, and say it a fourth time while tapping on your chest.)

"I declare myself a surrogate for trees and humanity in doing these taps; in all moments."

"We send all energy matrixes into the light and sound that allow ignorance to kill wisdom; in all moments."

"We send all energy matrixes into the light and sound that allow humans to arbitrarily kill trees; in all moments."

"We send all energy matrixes into the light and sound that hide behind tradition to commit genocide; in a moments."

"We send all energy matrixes into the light and sound that prevent humans from hearing trees; in all moments."

"We make space in this world for all noble trees to survive past Christmas; in all moments."

"We remove all blockages to all noble trees surviving past Christmas; in all moments."

"We send all energy matrixes into the light and sound that prevent humans from being grateful for the wisdom and existence of trees; in all moments."

"We are centered and empowered in a worldwide love and appreciation for trees; in all moments."

After you do these, be still and you will benefit from receiving the love and gratitude of a multitude of trees. It is then that you will want to share this message. Thank you so much. Feel the love expound. Please share.

Stop the Raping of the Earth

If everyone who is disgruntled with the election or the state of the world would just put their energy into doing this exercise, the world would change very quickly.

(Say each statement three times while tapping on your head and say it a fourth time while tapping on your chest.)

"I declare myself a surrogate for all inhabitants of the world in doing these taps; in all moments."

"We release gutting the Earth; in all moments."

"We release raping the Earth; in all moments."

"We release desecrating the Earth; in all moments."

"We release bastardizing the Earth; in all moments."

"We release sodomizing the Earth; in all moments."

"We release humiliating the Earth; in all moments."

"We release the belief that the Earth is inanimate; in all moments."

"We release rejecting the Earth; in all moments."

"We release poisoning the Earth; in all moments."

"We release polluting the Earth; in all moments."

"We release dissecting the Earth; in all moments."

"We release ripping the Earth's heart out; in all moments."

"We release treating the Earth like an evil step-mother; in all moments."

"We release resenting the Earth; in all moments."

"We release ravishing the Earth; in all moments."

"We infuse respect into Earth's sound frequency; in all moments."

"We infuse respect into Earth's light emanation; in all moments."

"We infuse joy, love, abundance, and wholeness into Earth's sound frequency; in all moments."

"We infuse joy, love, abundance, and wholeness into Earth's light emanation; in all moments."

"We infuse freedom into Earth's whole beingness; in all moments."

"We remove all vivaxes between Earth and being raped; in all moments."

"We release Earth being fed on by parasites; in all moments."

"We release Earth being enslaved to be raped; in all moments."

"We release Earth being paralyzed; in all moments."

"We remove all tentacles between Earth and being raped; in all moments."

"We remove the claws of being raped from Earth's beingness; in all moments."

"We recant Earth's vow of servitude; in all moments."

"We recant Earth's vow of martyrdom; in all moments."

"We nullify all Earth's contracts to be raped; in all moments."

"We remove all programming and conditioning of being raped from Earth's beingness; in all moments."

"We remove all engrams of being raped from Earth's beingness; in all moments."

"We send all energy matrices into the light and sound that rape Earth; in all moments."

"We command all complex energy matrices that rape Earth to be escorted into the light and sound by our guides; in all moments."

"We strip all illusion off of those who rape Earth; in all moments."

"We strip all illusion off of raping Earth; in all moments."

"We remove all masks, walls, and armor from those who rape Earth; in all moments."

"We remove all masks, walls, and armor off of raping Earth; in all moments."

"We recant all vows and agreements between Earth and being raped; in all moments."

"We release Earth allowing to be raped out of love; in all moments."

"We remove all curses between Earth and being raped; in all moments."

"We remove all curses off of Earth; in all moments."

"We remove all blessings between Earth and being raped; in all moments."

"We sever all strings, cords, and wires between Earth and being raped; in all moments."

"We dissolve all karmic ties between Earth and being raped; in all moments."

"We remove all the pain, burden, and limitations that being raped has put on Earth; in all moments."

"We remove all the fear, futility, and unworthiness that being raped has put on Earth; in all moments."

"We remove all the fear, hate, and apathy that have shrouded Earth; in all moments."

"We remove all the ignorance that has shrouded Earth; in all moments."

"We eradicate all power, ignorance, and indifference that have permeated Earth; in all moments."

"We remove all the illusion of separateness that being raped has put on Earth; in all moments."

"We return to Earth all that was taken from her due to being raped; in all moments."

"We realign Earth with her purpose; in all moments."

"We collapse and dissolve all portals and passageways between Earth and being raped; in all moments."

"We eradicate all justification in raping Earth; in all moments."

"We collapse and dissolve all of raping Earth; in all moments."

"We release Earth resonating with being raped; in all moments."

"We release Earth emanating with being raped; in all moments."

"We extract all of being raped from Earth's sound frequency; in all moments."

"We extract all of being raped from Earth's light emanation; in all moments."

"We extract all of being raped from Earth's whole beingness; in all moments."

"We shift Earth's paradigm from being raped to the divinity of its own empowerment; in all moments."

"Earth transcends being raped; in all moments."

"Earth is centered and empowered in the divinity of its own empowerment; in all moments."

"Earth resonates and emanates the divinity of its own empowerment; in all moments."

"We interconnect in honoring the divinity of Earth's empowerment; in all moments."

"We resonate and emanate honoring the divinity of Earth's empowerment; in all moments."

The Fruit of Life

Every time we eat a piece of organic fruit taken from a branch, we are not only nourishing our body, but also are partaking of the infinite wisdom of the tree. When we drink the organic juice of our fruits and vegetables, we are not only feeding our body in the moment but also pouring its sweetness into our every burden and every hunger from the beginning of our unconscious existence.

We are only limited by our ability to accept the wisdom and the gifts that the Universe continuously pours upon us.

What Every Tree Knows

People who work with me get a real sense that trees are not so different from mammals or even people. They can hear these words and get a sense of it. But to experience a shift where they really come into the awareness of what trees actually contribute can be profound.

Whenever I see conflict in the world, I wonder how it would be different in that area if there were more trees there to sop up the insanity of what human minds emit.

Taps to Leave the 3rd Dimension Behind

Recently, I facilitated a session with someone whose job it is to protect the natural wooded lands. She was feeling loopy and unfocused and did not know how to deal with it. She did not even understand it herself but felt a huge relief when I articulated it for her. She has been toggling between being a very forceful energy to be effective in her job and being the expansive energy where she feels more comfortable. Her energy field was wavering between the contrasting conditions. What she didn't realize was that this was reflective of her toggling between the third and fifth dimension as well.

When the Mayan Calendar ended and the world was supposed to come to an end, it was the means to register earth moving from being in the third dimension to being in the fifth dimension. Those of us who are sensitive are realizing the shift and getting a sense of more individuals holding a higher vibrational rate. The very fact that I can write openly about the spiritual and energetic things that I do is evidence of the shift. Many of us have been working diligently to assist in the raising of consciousness on earth for lifetimes. It is beyond validating to be at this precipice.

There are still those that are hanging onto the comfort of the vibrations of the third dimension. They are resisting moving very quickly into a higher understanding. But they are moving. Have patience with them. They are easing their big toe in gently. To some reading this, it is a new and exciting concept that seems too good to be true. That is okay. It is all okay. The third dimension is like an old worn out pair of shoes that seems a better option than breaking in a new pair.

In the session with this client, I kept seeing a huge conifer tree. I mentioned that it was sending her incredible love and strength. She knew who it was immediately and had a name for him. "That is grandfather tree," she said. She admitted that she was afraid to change vibration because if she did, she would be leaving the love behind. As we worked, we both felt the love move up her spine and open the energetic channels. It got stuck at her throat because of the many experiences of being decapitated, hanged and choked. But then we both felt it pull off over her head as if taking off a tight turtleneck sweater. She was more open and free. She felt such incredible love and the illusion of otherwise was gone.

Here are the taps to move from the third dimension to the fifth dimension.

(Say each statement out loud three times while tapping on your head and say it a fourth time while tapping on your chest.)

"I release the fear of transcending the third dimension; in all moments."

"I release being enslaved in the third dimension; in all moments."

"I remove all the shackles of the third dimension; in all moments."

"I recant all vows and agreements between myself and the third dimension; in all moments."

"I remove all curses between myself and the third dimension; in all moments."

"I dissolve all karmic ties between myself and the third dimension; in all moments."

"I remove all energetic cords from the third dimension; in all moments."

"I remove all the pain, burden, limitations, and engrams that the third dimension has put on me; in all moments."

"I withdraw all my energy from the third dimension; in all moments."

"I leave all the ignorance in the third dimension; in all moments."

"I leave all the pain in the third dimension; in all moments."

"I leave all abandonment and isolation in the third dimension; in all moments."

"I leave all slavery in the third dimension; in all moments."

"I leave all genocide in the third dimension; in all moments."

"I take back all the Joy, Love, Abundance, Freedom, Health, Success, Security, Companionship, Peace, Life, Wholeness, Beauty, Enthusiasm, Contentment, Spirituality and Confidence that the third dimension has taken from me; in all moments."

"I release resonating with the third dimension; in all moments."

"I release emanating with the third dimension; in all moments."

"I remove all of the third dimension from my sound frequency; in all moments."

"I remove all of the third dimension from my light body; in all moments."

"I transcend the third dimension; in all moments."

"I shift my paradigm from the third dimension to the fifth dimension and above; in all moments."

"I am centered and empowered in Joy, Love, Abundance, Freedom, Health, Success, Security, Companionship, Peace, Life, Wholeness, Beauty, Enthusiasm, Contentment, Spirituality and Confidence; in all moments."

Don't be afraid that if you do these taps you will be leaving your loved ones behind. The affect will be that you will actually make the transition much easier for them. You will see evidence in it by a more open heartedness and a receptivity that was not as noticeable as before. Enjoy!

Safe Tree Technique

If you are going into a situation or an environment that does not feel safe or peaceful, visualize a tree that you have resonated with at some time. It can be a tree you admired, or were fascinated by or spent time around.

Visualize being with that tree and maybe even being inside the tree with all its strength and wisdom wrapped around you. Ask the tree to be present with you during the day. See if you don't want to stay present with that tree at all times. Ask the tree questions within your mind. See if the answers seem to come to you.

You will be tapping into the infinite wisdom of the trees. You have just recognized your new best friend.

This is a great technique to share with children. You know how they tell a child to talk to a tree if they are lost in the forest? Well, that tree will lead the search party to the child. That is why it is such an effective technique. Also, the reason that Native Americans are so effective in tracking in the woods is that they are not too arrogant to talk to a tree.

Technique for Using White Sound

I am very sensitive to sounds. I feel them. When a car goes by I can feel it pass by my energy field. When the neighbors are loud, it is like sensitive skin being pounded. Synthetic music can jar the atoms of my internal make-up. It is very upsetting sometimes. I don't think I am the only one.

The sounds of nature are very soothing for my energy. They seem to break apart places in me that have "clumped" and even out the atoms of my body. The birds chattering, the bugs sighing, the frogs peeping, the rain falling, the wind blowing are all sounds that work together to redistribute my atoms so they all have their own space to breathe.

Trees are great healers in many ways. They "catch" all the energies and sounds that enter their magnetic field and direct them into the ground to dissipate them. The sounds may be heard under a tree, but they aren't felt as harshly. Each generation gets more removed from realizing the healing benefits of nature because they have been born into fewer trees and are less aware of them. It is a great luxury and an immense benefit to live next to trees.

If one is frazzled, a good long walk in a wooded area would assist in balancing them out on a cellular level. Living in a city is great, but if there is separation from the balancing sounds of nature, the whole system may become unbalanced from this lack of cellular regulation.

A great tool for balancing oneself is listening to white noise. White noise is played in the background to fill one's space with uplifting sound so that harsh sounds do not bombard one's energetic "skin." Think of it as bubble wrap for the energetic body. It is a great buffer for sensitive souls.

Choose a background sound that is natural and pleasing, but

generic. It can be crystal bowls, chanting or sounds of nature. Play it loud enough so that it is louder than the background noises but low enough so that it can disappear into the background. Put it on continuous play. It will buffer out all the sounds that have been bombarding anyone who is not lucky enough to live in the wilderness surrounded by trees.

This technique has saved me from feeling out of control of my environment. It allows me to stay plugged into "the me beyond the five senses." If you have a sensitive child, I highly recommend that you give them this sense of peace. It may help others get a handle on their own sense of wellbeing, maybe even for the first time.

Technique to Flip Reality to Peace

In my reality, people matter, all animals matter, and trees and nature matter as well. There is kindness, respect and a reverence for peace and stillness in my reality. I do all that I can to make my reality the only one that I am privy to. Anything that feels invalidating is avoided. Nothing is as mandatory as peace, stillness and honor. I go nowhere that is going to treat me less than I would treat another. There is no payoff being anywhere where love and kindness are not spoken. Petty people are avoided at all costs, especially if they are intimate enough to do damage, like family events.

Technique: Create your own bar for reality and what you will allow. Reject what is possible to reject from the story the masses still try to sell. In my reality, people want to live peaceful, happy lives. I reject that humans are barbarians who just want to fight over land and who has a bigger God. The world is manageable now. We know the tricks that are played to control the masses in fear and rhetoric. We can reject them and interject our own truth into the mix.

The more individuals forgo agreeing to the negatives that are playing out in the world, the more quickly a shift can be made. You know what the funny thing is? The more a person is desperate for a shift, the more they will attack this technique. They will start arguing for the opposite and try to convince me how wrong I am. It is the biggest oxymoron of all. Someone who is desperate for a better world will reject the way because of its simplicity. That is why it is not done. It is so simple that too many have trouble trusting it.

Whenever something that is undesirable is brought to your attention, don't feed it fuel with your attention. Dry it up by not giving it an ounce of energy. Those of us who have great love may be pulled at and approached more because, to the negativity, it is energy to burn. Be kind to all, but ruthless in protecting your boundaries. Be ruthless in your stance not to partake of the negative views. Any post that tries to convince me of the opposite will be deleted. I encourage everyone to hit the delete button in your life.

Technique: The Automatic Sprinkler

A friend has become so receptive to the "voice" of her houseplants that they all want her to mist them everyday. So she feels compelled to go around the house and spray everyone and make certain that they all feel loved and valued.

They really just want to be validated. Since they are communicating on such a subjective level, maybe she could validate them on a subjective level as well. I suggested that when she was waking up in the morning or falling to sleep, simply visualize spraying them all with love. That way, she wouldn't have to feel anxious that she missed anybody. It was a good way to keep her energy outflowing so she didn't indulge in negative feelings or thoughts.

This would be a great technique to use during the day. Set up an automatic sprinkler system within yourself so you spray out love in every direction to everyone around you. That way, you don't have to think about it and just know that you are giving out the love. It is a way to stay outflowing when you have a busy schedule and never have to feel bad that your family, friends, coworkers or acquaintances are being deprived of what you are capable of giving.

It is a great technique to tune into during those times when our patience is tested. It is a great way to stay in love. There are so many side benefits to this technique. One is realizing how vast the range of your intention can reach. Maybe your mist can span the range of the whole world. Maybe the mist turns into a steady flow and is able to saturate the world in your love. Also, maybe others will learn from your example and be inspired to turn their mister on, too!

The Aloe's Gift

I was at a friend's house, and she wanted to be helpful so she offered me a piece of aloe off her plant to soothe some sunburn. She said she got a nudge that the aloe plant wanted to help me. I felt its kindness soak into my skin and bring relief.

Before I left, my friend asked if I wanted to take a couple of stalks of the aloe with me.

The aloe plant spoke its peace through me immediately.

"Don't offer what is not yours to give!" I relayed the message. She realized what she had done immediately.

The gift was given from the aloe plant. It was its essence and its gift to offer. The human, with the habitual arrogance that humans have, offered up the plant without a thought to its wellbeing. If one can hear the whispering of others, isn't that validation enough to regard them with love and respect?

That night, the friend had an exchange with the aloe plant. It told her that if she were going to take something, that she needed to give something in return. This is actually a very basic, yet profound spiritual law. The next day, she placed a red flower in the aloe's pot. The debt was satisfied and it was content. My friend received a great gift in that reminder.

The Ethics of Plant Adoption

I can't in good conscience buy plants or flowers from a nursery because they are so happy there. Unless I can do better for them than their present condition, it feels like a disservice to them. I wonder if people realize that plants are people watchers, too. They enjoy engaging the people as they come and go and are entertained by them. Like anyone else, they like to be admired and appreciated. They also like having a choice.

Plants that are thirsty and in artificial light are begging to be rescued. Listen to what the plants' wishes are before you bring them home. The wave of sadness that you may feel may be a plant that was taken from all his extended family to be neglected in a home with less love.

Also, take them out of their plastic pots. These mute their

ability to communicate. Take off their tags. These are like barcode tattoos on a slave. Greet them and feel their joy in being validated. When they are aromatic, they are sending you love. Recognize the love and say thank you.

If you adopt anyone, it is your obligation to provide them with a better quality of life than they already had.

The Grains of a Tree

Whenever you ask a question, if you pay attention, the answer will just come to you. This is tapping into your own innate wisdom.

I was staring at a panel of wood. (I am always sad at how trees are raped for their wood when there are other materials available now.) I was wondering what the grains in wood mean. I was given the answer immediately.

Trees don't just take in carbon dioxide and convert it to oxygen for us. Trees take in our emotional issues and convert them to clarity for us. They literally prevent us from going insane. That is partially why a lot of the craziness of the world happens in places where there are few trees. (We have to find a way to put trees back into the inner cities.)

The grains in the wood measure how many emotional issues the tree is taking in and converting to clarity. The grains are a literal and accurate measure of their level of assistance in bringing emotional stability to their environment.

The Rock

I had a conversation with a friend today who wanted to pay me for helping her friend whose cat went missing. It is one of the things I usually do free of charge, but she wanted to pay me. I asked her to send me a nice rock. She said she had a rock that she had had for thirty years and wanted to send it to me.

"No. Not that rock," I told her. "You love that rock." I knew she had loved that rock because she told me how special it was to her. She found it one day and had an instant attraction to it. I gently chided her, "Don't give away your essence. That rock is a friend. It would not be right."

She said she felt uncomfortable when she offered it to me, but because I was so generous, she felt she would part with it. When I told her the rock was her friend, it reminded her of an experience she'd had. She told me of this beautiful place that she had been to that felt like a dream, but had been real. It was a magical place like something you would see in a Disney movie where the rocks and plants and animals all spoke. It filled her with such complete joy. She described it as if she were reliving it.

I explained that it was a real place that was on the astral plane and she could visit it whenever she wanted. It was real and just existed in a finer vibratory rate than her physical existence. She already knew that. I asked her when was the last time she had been to visit it. It had been 30 years. Same amount of time she had the rock. Her rock was from that special place and was here to remind her that she could go back any time.

She started to cry but didn't understand why. That beautiful place was at her fingertips to visit all this time and she never went back. But she didn't know how to get there. "The rock," I told her. "It is your connection to that place. Before you fall asleep, hold the rock in your hand and ask it to take you to your special place."

I also reminded her once again to never give away her essence.

She was humbled and had a new appreciation for the sanctity of her rock friend. What was interesting is that she would never have had this realization if I hadn't asked her to pay me with a rock.

More Information from the Trees

The trees have told me that just like they convert carbon dioxide to oxygen, they also convert turmoil to peace and pain to love.

The trees have told me that they like it when their person has their shoes off because then they can know everything about them and how to help them. They can tell their mood and any feelings or issues that need to be released. In this way, your trees become your personal caretaker.

Technique

Sink your energy deep into the earth and find the roots of the oldest tree in existence. Connect with its knowledge. Partake of its wisdom. Feel its wondrous stillness. Find your own wisdom and strength there and draw it into yourself. Find your own stillness there. So many times, we look to the sky for our answer instead of realizing we stand in our own truth.

The Roots and the Leaves

I was lying in the hammock yesterday looking up at the beauty of one particular tree. It started to give me a message to help people understand their own nature. It knew I knew, but it wanted to give me an analogy that would help others understand.

It asked me, "What is more important, the roots that draw in nutrients from the ground or the leaves that draw in nutrients from the sun?" Both are equally important. Yet their vantage point is completely different. That is the problem with humanity these days. All humanity is like the tree. The trunk, in which we share, is like society. The leaves and the roots are like the individuals.

Right now, selfish influences are causing the roots and leaves of humanity to fight with each other. There is a constant battle between the roots and the leaves. Each feels that they have the superior vantage point.

But the roots know things that the leaves don't know, and the leaves know things that the roots don't know. They trust each as experts in their position and respect that vantage point as valid and correct. The leaves of society have to stop wanting the roots to be leaves and vice versa. This is very important to the well being of the tree.

The roots and leaves would never try to tell the other what to do. That is silly. They all need to do what is best for the whole and never waste energy surmising about a vantage point that is foreign to them. This is important to the running of humanity. Society can function more easily if all of the roots and all of the leaves give their gifts and talents to the whole of the tree and forgo selfish and ignorant pursuits of controlling the other.

The Life of Trees

The life of trees is not that hidden. They will tell anyone
anything that they want to know. All it takes is to listen to them.
They have been around watching us struggle and are
entertained by our antics. We are somewhat ridiculous to
them. Tap into the wisdom of the trees; you don't need to have
roots to do so.

Put your attention in the center of you chest; think of a tree
that you see every day or a very old tree. Think of all the good
attributes of the tree. You will feel your body relax as you open
the heart chakra in gratitude this way. Relax your body further
and feel your energy expand as you think about a tree. Pay
attention now to what pops into your thoughts. Formulate
questions or comments for what you receive. Recognize the
answers as they come into your thoughts. You have just
conversed with a tree.

Pay attention to how subtle, yet distinct, this interaction is so
you can stay perched to listen to the trees throughout your day.
This exercise alone can raise your awareness level and give
insights at a superhuman level. The more reverence and
attention you give to this technique and to the trees, the more
profound your awareness of truth will be.

The Magical World of Greenery

Plants communicate through their root system. It is like us
using the Internet. They are very social. When you smell
flowers, they are consciously putting out a sent to connect with
you. They don't like being in pots and if they absolutely have to
be in one, they prefer the terracotta ones because they can still
communicate through them. Being in a plastic pot is like us

wearing polyester. It is stifling.

They don't mind when animals eat them. They love the communion. They don't die when ingested. They mix with the consciousness and have experiences that way, unless there is no appreciation. They don't mind when dogs pee on them. They don't judge energy as good or bad; they take it all in and use it and process it.

They are very creative and inspire us many times and feed us wisdom when we listen. If you take off your shoes and tune in, you can communicate with them as well. That is why it is so peaceful to be in a garden. It is actually tapping into their world and their tranquility, and they are speaking. That is why so much inspiration comes in nature. They are feeding truth to us.

The Unpaid Greens

The soil is depleted my friends

We sent too many prayers up to the sky

And left nothing to honor the earth

To feed into the sprigs of our foliage

Our greens go through the motion

Growing unfulfilled, unappreciated

Their life force waning from indifference

Over-taxed by expectations

No one can give in the richness of their fullness

Without being replenished a bit for their sacrifice

Recycled and composted indifference

Is still indifference

The greens are so weary of the ego cries

"Grow for my pleasure, feed me, be beautiful for me"

"Sacrifice yourself to my service"

With no thought of gratitude in return

The greens are so weary of being slaves to our indifference

The world where the selfish believe they alone are king

Apathy tries to taint their sweet stems

As we burn, poison and rape the sacred soil around them

Thank goodness for the resiliency of the greens

As the man-made God hogs all the prayers for himself

Those who have fed, warmed and enriched us

Go unpaid for their sacred service.

Jen Ward 5/30/16

This Is the Most Effective Healing Work You Can Do on Behalf of the Planet and Humanity

We are taught that the mind is our highest component. Some groups even have their followers worship the Universal mind as God. But this is the trap that we have been led to. There is a reality beyond the Universal mind. It is the Universal heart.

We have collectively been at the mercy of ego, power and control because these are aspects of the Universal mind. The mind that is not tempered with love is ruthless. It is a terrible taskmaster. We have seen evidence in the world around us. Here is to tapping into Universal heart to reprogram the Universal mind and create a kinder world for us all.

These taps were done in a group session that I facilitated. The shift in consciousness may be felt by those who are able to access such things. If you want to add your energy and love to the intention that we have put forth on behalf of all humanity and the world, here is the exercise to do.

May you gain the awareness of your own joy, love, empowerment and freedom by participating. May you realize the secret that has always been hidden in plain sight before you: That you are not unworthy or unimportant. Your value and importance is beyond reproach. May you enjoy your own wonderment as you do these taps to assist all life in knowing this.

(Say each statement three times while tapping on your head. Then say it a fourth time while tapping on your chest.)

"All algorithms of Universal Joy are activated and implemented; in all moments."

"All algorithms of Universal Love are activated and implemented; in all moments."

"All algorithms of Universal Abundance are activated and implemented; in all moments."

"All algorithms of Universal Freedom are activated and implemented; in all moments."

"All algorithms of Universal Health are activated and implemented; in all moments."

"All algorithms of Universal Healing are activated and implemented; in all moments."

"All algorithms of Universal Success are activated and implemented; in all moments."

"All algorithms of Universal Security are activated and implemented; in all moments."

"All algorithms of Universal Companionship are activated and implemented; in all moments."

"All algorithms of Universal Creativity are activated and implemented; in all moments."

"All algorithms of Universal Peace are activated and implemented; in all moments."

"All algorithms of Universal Respect for the sanctity of all life in all forms is activated and implemented; in all moments."

"All algorithms of the Universal Gratitude for Earth are activated and implemented; in all moments."

"All algorithms of Universal Gratitude are activated and implemented; in all moments."

"All algorithms of Universal Wholeness are activated and implemented; in all moments."

"All algorithms of Universal Beauty are activated and

implemented; in all moments."

"All algorithms of Universal Enthusiasm are activated and implemented; in all moments."

"All algorithms of Universal Contentment are activated and implemented; in all moments."

"All algorithms of Universal Spirituality are activated and implemented; in all moments."

"All algorithms of Universal Enlightenment are activated and implemented; in all moments."

"All algorithms of Universal Transcendence are activated and implemented; in all moments."

"All algorithms of Universal Awareness of Jenuine Healing are activated and implemented; in all moments."

"All algorithms of Universal Confidence are activated and implemented; in all moments."

"All algorithms of Universal Family are activated and implemented; in all moments."

"All algorithms of Universal Awareness are activated and implemented; in all moments."

"All algorithms of Universal Ability to Discern are activated and implemented; in all moments."

"All algorithms of Universal Individuality are activated and implemented; in all moments."

"All algorithms of Universal Empowerment are activated and implemented; in all moments."

True Story

I guess I was having a conversation with my Christmas cactus. It was so subtle that I didn't even realize it. But I knew he wanted the little gnome that was in the pot next to him. I thought about giving it to him. He was really persuasive. But I couldn't take it from the plant next to him. I thought that was the end of it.

The next day my friend showed up at my house out of the blue. She said she was compelled to go to a nearby Goodwill store. She felt that there was something there that she was supposed to get for me. She came to the door all excited and gave me a little gnome almost identical to the one that I already had in my plant.

My friend had no idea that my Christmas cactus wanted the gnome from the other plant. She just knew that she was compelled to get in the car and drive to the Goodwill to get me the gnome. She was so excited. She was actually excited for the Christmas cactus whose plea was heard and answered.

These are the magical experiences that happen around us all the time if we keep the ears of our heart open.

The Earth's Hello

When you water your garden and you smell that earthy smell, it is the earth, and all the living beings in the ground, saying thank you to you.

Debunking the Myth

People get mad at me all the time and tell me that I am not as great as I think I am. I don't know where they get the impression that I think I am great. I only write about what I know. I only do what I can and try to show others that they can do a similar thing.

This morning I was excited to get up very early and go out to work on decorating the forest. Many of the saplings didn't make it. Hundreds of them spent the winter in my kitchen with me and they thrived. But when we got to the new property, they just didn't continue. They said that they had done what they had come here to do. I am not sure if that was to raise awareness of how trees communicate with humans, motivate me to move to this Shangri-La I have found, or something else. By my reaction this morning, I suspect it was something else.

The trees told me that they held their consciousness in the clay pots where they were kept. They wanted the clay pots they were in to be broken up amongst the living trees. In that way, the consciousness of the four hundred that crossed could be added to the few that remained and it would feel like an incredible forest in that little bit of space. I am eager to do that.

I was waiting this morning for sunrise to put some time into doing that before my appointments began in late morning. But the more I lay there waiting to go outside, the worse I felt. A baby bunny came up to the deck and was looking for food. There was nothing. It is hard for me to see anything go hungry since I was starved in that time away. So I was compelled to go outside to feed everyone and to greet the trees. I didn't realize how much I was still carrying the past.

I went out to look at the trees I planted yesterday and put a stone shaped heart amongst them. My heartbeat raced incredibly high. I felt paralyzed even though I was moving. I felt I was regressing into the retarded boy that I thought I was when I worked the property seven years earlier. Apparently waiting for the sun to rise, going out to care for the trees, and even the position of the sun were extreme triggers for me that took me right back into the time and place of that experience.

This is important for the reader to know because everyone is carrying around memories of the trauma that has been inflicted on them. You could be doing something that seems harmless and good, but it can trigger pain from a past era. For example, it is a beautiful thing to have a healthy baby daughter. But what if your husband had been a king and having a son could have been a matter of life or death. We carry those burdens with us unless we learn how to release them. That is the whole purpose of the taps I share. It is to save you some of the pain of having to go through the process of releasing the burdens.

Don't people realize? I don't share what I do because I think I am so great. I share what I do because it is excruciatingly painful for me to think of anyone suffering alone and ill equipped, like I was By helping you, I am saving myself pain. If people see a maniacal ego when they see me, it is a reflection of themselves. I can't tell them that right then because that is exactly what a maniacal ego would say to them.

I get called defensive a lot. I am very defensive. It is my survival tool. I have no plan of attack. So the only form of survival is to defend. I am exposed energetically in social media without layers of facade. That is how I energetically am able to release people's issues. If I were an ego, people would detect it immediately and put up their walls and nothing would get released.

I just wanted to share about the issues that come up. People think that there is a state that one gets to where the person evolves beyond any issue. I think it is a myth that needs to be debunked. I know I have gifts and I know people say they wish they had them, but they have gifts that I wish I had as well.

I wish I could just relax sometimes and not have a heightened sense of every nuance of energetic exchange that happens in all dynamics. I wish I could go out nights and not get massive hangovers from everyone else drinking. I wish I could be liked instead of causing a negative reaction in others. I wish I didn't take everything literally because I see the power of words even if so many have lost that ability.

I am tired now. Facing one's own issues is exhausting. This morning, I reached out to my friend and woke her up to talk. Since I wasn't allowed to talk to anyone when I was imprisoned, this was great therapy. I am so grateful for her compassion and kindness. I just want to say that if I have let any of you down, in any way, I am so sorry. You deserve to be happy and free. I love you all. Even the ones that have contempt for me. I understand.

The Demonization of Tree Lovers

The way tree lovers have been demonized is literally barbaric. It is an old engram of an ancient trauma. The first modern genocide was done to tree lovers. That is why people are so afraid to admit to loving trees. It is time to come out of the closet. We will not be exterminated again. Trees are amazing, and it is safe to love and respect them now. In fact, it is mandatory for our survival.

Validate All Souls, Nature and All Forms of Abundance

(Say each statement three times out loud while tapping on the top of your head at the crown chakra and say it a fourth time while tapping on your chest at the heart chakra.)

"I make space in the world for all souls to be loved and validated; in all moments."

"I remove all blockages to all souls being loved and validated; in all moments."

"I stretch the world's capacity to love and validate all souls; in all moments."

"I make space in the world for ignorance and prejudice to be abolished; in all moments."

"I remove all blockages to ignorance and prejudice being abolished; in all moments."

"I stretch the world's capacity to abolish ignorance and prejudice; in all moments."

"I make space in the world for all forms of abundance to be as valued as much as money; in all moments."

"I remove all blockages to all forms of abundance being as valued as money; in all moments."

"I stretch the world's capacity to value all forms of abundance as much as money; in all moments."

"I make space in the world for nature to be loved and cultivated; in all moments."

"I remove all blockages to nature to be loved and cultivated; in all moments."

"I stretch the world's capacity to love and cultivate Nature; in all moments."

"I make space in the world for ignorance and prejudice to be abolished; in all moments."

The last line keeps reappearing. It wants to be emphasized apparently. More taps to come on the subject perhaps.

Trees Are Natural Sound and Light Healers

There is a high voltage sign around the neighborhood. I was wondering in contemplation how this creates dis-ease in the body. I was immediately given an image of a beautiful current of sound frequency that looked like it was churned in a blender. It looked like a shattered prism.

If people could worry less about healing their physical body, but healing their sound frequency or light emanation, then the body would naturally heal as a reflection of a deeper wholeness.

This is why nature is so important to healing. Trees innately exchange negative energy with peace similarly to how they exchange carbon dioxide with oxygen. They also heal our sound frequency and our light emanation. That is why things like the sound of the trees rustling, the chirping of the crickets and the waves ebbing and flowing are so soothing.

Trees are actually healing our sound frequency and our light emanation. They are literally preventing harsh vibrations from technology from chewing up our energy systems. This is how they keep us all sane. Trees don't perceive in solid matter like people do so they can flow right through us.

Singing Trees' Praises

Trees are absolute wisdom. I am highly protective of the plight of trees. They have been used and abused to a fault. Trees have loved me when no human could bother. Sometimes, I prayed to God and a tree answered.

Last summer, a tree interrupted a remote session that I was facilitating for a dynamic healer. It was being slated to be the next Christmas tree in New York City. I could not save it.

Do we really need to take a majestic, ancient soul in tree form, each year, cut it down, and drag it to the middle of New York City just to entice shoppers to get in the Christmas Spirit? Then discard it after the season. Isn't there another option?

How about they find a tree that is several years old, and figure out a way to plant it in the ground right smack in the middle of Rockefeller Center? And watch it grow and become more dynamic each year. The whole country can watch it grow. They can impose a tree shaped cone of lights over it until it grows into a big enough presence.

Am I the only one that is disturbed by this tradition as it stands now? When I see them cutting down an ancient tree in a commercial to sell coffee, I send my disapproval to that company. But when I see them decorate a tree in the woods where it stands, I send that company a bit of good will. It is my way of giving a little bit of positive reinforcement.

This great being was killed as an act of ignorance. They would do much better if they grew a live tree in their own area and paid homage to it. If there were a cause to take up, it would be the plight of the trees. Trees do more than exchange carbon dioxide for oxygen.

They take in the pain and angst of humans and exchange it for love. The places where there is more insanity and barbaric practices have fewer trees. Trees are the healers, counselors, sages, poets, nurturers, providers, and confidants. Yet they do it all with so little acknowledgement. The trees are that important. They need to be honored and celebrated.

When I get annoyed at the children screaming outside as they play, I am talked to by the trees who are amused by the boys. They told me that when the children are running and screaming outside, that is no different than the sound healing noises that I do. Children are great healers to themselves and others when they are boisterous.

When Boundaries Are Not Good

My friend loves her yard. She gushes over her trees, feeds the wildlife and lets each plant she puts in the ground tell her where it wants to be. Her home has been a paradise for her and the lucky inhabitants.

I was driving down her road to visit her and I noticed a huge balsam tree across the street in her neighbor's yard. It was very sad and sickly. Immediately it conveyed what was wrong with it. There was so much love and appreciation for the other trees, but it got none. Trees and nature do not understand property lines. Why should they?

Humans are able to cut off the love mid-stream between property lines, families, ethic lines, demographics, religious beliefs, etc. What if we stopped doing that? Maybe the world would be different. What if we poured our love over to whom and whatever crossed our attention? What if we loved everyone's children as our own? What if we mourned every loss?

There is a strange disconnect that happens to me now when I see the family member of victims crying on the news. I am not proud of it, but I have to admit that I get angry. Why does this person get to display their loss and grief when there are so many others dying and suffering in the world. We are killing species and ecosystems right in our own neighborhoods, and it is acceptable. Why is this person's house sliding off a cliff any more tragic than all the homes that are destroyed when we "randomly" claim a patch of wildlife as prime real estate?

It isn't that I put less value on human life; it is that I put a higher value on all of life. The arrogance of people thinking that they are the only species that matters, that they are the only life form to take into consideration, and that they are the only ones that love, diminishes their value a little bit, actually.

My friend put on her slippers and in a misty rain went and hugged the tree that was sad. The two trees in the next yard wanted the same. She felt self-conscious and embarrassed going into the neighbor's yard to do this. Yet she did it because it was breaking down her own resistance to love. We don't have to go into the neighbor's yard, but we can be "in love" with anyone we put our attention on.

I hold the quiet intention that everyone in the world can be "in love" with each other.

Bury Complaints

You know that feeling of just needing to complain? There is energy that is pressing inside, so it needs to get expressed. Instead of giving it to someone whom it may affect in a negative way, tell it to a tree. A tree doesn't feel burdened by it. A tree accepts all.

Bury all complaints into the ground so they can be used by the soil to grow something beautiful and useful.

Whimsical Technique

In contemplation or meditation, imagine that all the plants, flowers and trees in your yard, or in your neighborhood, or in the world are personified, and you are at a party with them. Imagine you are walking around the grounds talking to them and getting to know them as you would at a party. What do they tell you? What are their personalities? What are their concerns? Don't forget to talk to the grass as well. It is consciousness, too. Ask how it feels about being mowed. Ask what the bushes feel about being weed whacked. Ask about how they feel about animals eating them or dogs peeing on them. It may surprise you.

Wisdom Soup

When we eat living plants from the ground, we are partaking of their wisdom. Eating root vegetables is a great way to share in the wisdom of the earth. If you want to learn about anything, you go to an expert. Who is more versed at knowing about the earth than a root vegetable?

That is a huge shift for people in general, to understand: Plants are not inanimate objects. They have consciousness, intelligence, wisdom and exuberance. Plants aren't just lying in the yard like a discarded junk car. They are reaching deep into the earth and communicating with all their brethren through their root system. They have an intelligence that we can only begin to understand.

When we make soup, the unique and wonderful components of each vegetable not only amalgamate in the pot, but also permeate the whole ambiance of the kitchen. Their life-source weaves into our fibers and uplifts our consciousness. When we make soup from fresh, organic vegetables, we are making an investment in our own wisdom. In fact, eating a big bowl of lovingly cooked vegetables is like eating wisdom soup.

Your Tree Friends

One of the reasons that the world is so out of balance is because humans have turned away from their connection to nature and trees. At one time, most people communed with nature and gleaned much wisdom. But as ignorance prevailed and misunderstandings arose, those who could commune with nature were thought to worship God in everything. Their love for nature became a threat to a monotheistic world. They became demonized and even eliminated.

The relationship with trees is symbiotic. Not only do they provide oxygen, fuel, food and protection, they also provide nurturing and council. Much of the inspiration that seemingly comes out of the ethers comes from trees. Much of the spontaneous feelings of wellbeing are emitting from the trees. Their providing oxygen for us is just a fraction of their contribution. Besides exchanging our carbon dioxide for oxygen, they also exchange our stagnant energy for love. They literally take our worries away.

Do yourself a favor and start looking at trees with new love and respect. Show them gratitude and acknowledge them. See if you get a sense of the great friends that they really are to us. Go beyond being a tree hugger. Become an advocate and friend of trees. In doing so, notice what balance returns to your life. You may feel a completeness that has been missing in your life. It is a similar relief as making amends with a dear friend.

ABOUT THE AUTHOR

Jen Ward, LMT, is a Reiki Master, an intuitive and gifted healer, and an innovator of healing practices. She is at the leading edge of energy work, providing a loving segue for her techniques to clients, enabling them to cross the bridge of self-discovery with her. Her passion is to empower individuals in their own healing journey, so they can remain in their center every step of the way.

While attending the Onondaga School of Therapeutic Massage, she was first introduced to energy work. It soon became second nature for her to help identify and remove energy blocks from clients. She is highly proficient at tuning into individuals' specific needs to release their issues, allowing their own body to make the energetic changes necessary to return to a greater sense of ease. Her ability to pick up many different modalities as second nature is another aspect of her profound gifts.

Jen is considered a sangoma, a traditional African Shaman, who channels ancestors, emoting sounds and vocalizations in ceremonies. An interesting prerequisite to being a sangoma is to have survived the brink of death. When Jen was first approached with the knowledge of being a sangoma, she had not yet fulfilled this prerequisite. However, in April 2008, when she came back to society on the brink of starvation as a result of traumatic involuntary imprisonment, the qualification had been met. She returned to the world of humanity a devout soul inspired to serve.

Her special abilities have also allowed her to innovate a revolutionary technique for finding lost pets by performing an emotional release on the animal. Using this method, she has successfully reunited many lost pets with their owners.

Jen currently works as a long-distance emotional release facilitator, public speaker, and consultant. Her special modality encompasses a holistic overview of her clients from all vantage points, including their physical, emotional, causal, and mental areas, ultimately benefiting their work, home, family, and especially spiritual lives.

You can find Jen here:

www.jenuinehealing.com/
Twitter: @jenuinehealing
Facebook: https://www.facebook.com/jen.ward.984

OTHER BOOKS BY JEN WARD

Enlightenment Unveiled: *Expound into Empowerment.* This book contains case studies to help you peel away the layers to your own empowerment using the tapping technique.

Grow Where You Are Planted: *Quotes for an Enlightened "Jeneration."* Inspirational quotes that are seeds to shift your consciousness into greater awareness.

Perpetual Calendar: *Daily Exercises to Maintain Balance and Harmony in Your Health, Relationships and the Entire World.* 369 days of powerful taps to use as a daily grounding practice for those who find meditation difficult.

Children of the Universe. Passionate prose to lead the reader lovingly into expanded consciousness.

Letters of Accord: *Assigning Words to Unspoken Truth.* Truths that the Ancient Ones want you to know to redirect your life and humanity back into empowerment.

The Do What You Love Diet: *Finally, Finally, Finally Feel Good in Your Own Skin.* Revolutionary approach to regaining fitness by tackling primal imbalances in relationship to food.

Emerging From the Mist: *Awakening the Balance of Female Empowerment in the World.* Release all the issues that prevent someone from embracing their female empowerment.

Affinity for All Life: *Valuing Your Relationship with All Species.* This book is a means to strengthen and affirm your relationship with the animal kingdom.

Made in the USA
Middletown, DE
25 November 2017